BECOMING FUTURE YOU

Be the Hero of Your Own Life

MEL JOLLY

Copyright © 2021 by Author Rx, LLC

For permission requests, speaking inquiries, and bulk purchase bulk-purchase options, email melissa@authorrx.com.

Copyright Information

BECOMING FUTURE YOU

Cover designed by Meg Murrey's Designs

Interior designed by Mel Jolly

Edited by Tawdra Kandle

Proofread by Victory Editing and Lisa Hughey

All Rights Reserved. No part of this book may be reproduced by any process (mechanical, electronic, photographic, phonographic) or otherwise copied for private or public use without written permission from the author except for "fair use" as brief quotations embodied in reviews or articles.

The author of this book does not dispense medical, legal, tax, or other professional advice or prescribe the use of any technique, directly or indirectly, as a treatment for medical, emotional, physical, or psychological problems without the oversight or advice of a physician or qualified professional. The author's intent is to offer information of a general nature that may help you in your journey of improving your overall well-being. Your actions are your own. In the event you use any of the information in this book, the author and the publisher assume no responsibility for your actions.

This is work of nonfiction. While stories about the author's coaching clients and students have been included, identifying characteristics have been changed to protect the privacy of those individuals. Any resulting resemblance to individuals living or dead is entirely coincidental and unintentional.

❦ Created with Vellum

AUTHOR'S NOTE

1. In writing this book, it became evident I was going to have to pick a gender pronoun for Future You lest we all have to deal with me using "Future You" more times than any of us could handle. I chose "she," but if you use a different pronoun, that doesn't mean this book isn't for you. Just switch out all the "shes" for the appropriate pronoun, okay?
2. Of course I changed the names to protect the innocent (and the guilty). I'm not a monster.
3. I made a companion journal for you, which you can download for free at becomingfutureyou.com/book.

For the toughest woman I've ever known, my Babcia.

Thanks for teaching me to get up.

CONTENTS

Author's Note — 1

Part One
ACT I: INTRODUCING THE HERO... YOU!

1. Chapter 1: Call to Adventure — 9
2. Chapter 2: Who Are You Becoming? — 17
3. Chapter 3: It's Not about You — 31
4. Chapter 4: The Journey Is the Point — 41

Part Two
ACT II: VISION IS CREATED

5. Chapter 5: The Enemies Close In — 53
6. Chapter 6: Who's Directing This Movie? — 70
7. Chapter 7: Future You, the Superhero — 77
8. Chapter 8: The Villain Attacks — 88
9. Chapter 9: Unlocking & Embracing Your Powers — 102
10. Chapter 10: The Mission — 112

Part Three
ACT III: BECOMING FUTURE YOU

11. Chapter 11: Stepping into the Role — 131
12. Chapter 12: Habits — 139
13. Chapter 13: Stop Sabotaging Future You — 151
14. Chapter 14: Enjoying the Journey — 162
15. Chapter 15: You Are Ready — 179

Acknowledgments — 187

ACT I: INTRODUCING THE HERO... YOU!

CHAPTER 1: CALL TO ADVENTURE

Hey, you! We're going to change the way you think about your future.

This is not just another follow-your-dreams goals book or a stronger, better, faster book. This is a book about you and what you want. Even if you don't know what you want… yet.

You are the hero of this story.

You can reduce your stress and improve your finances; you can have supportive relationships and more time for hobbies (remember those?) and fun. You can live a meaningful, joyful, purposeful life if you'll stop thinking so much about what you *should* want and start thinking about what you *actually* want.

The first step is to stop thinking so much about what you're supposed to do and open your heart to what you desire. You have gifts and talents and superpowers, but you're not using them to their full extent. You've only scratched the surface of your capabilities.

Your goals and dreams and desires have been instilled in your heart for a reason. You're meant to chase them. Doing so will take you places you never thought you'd go, introduce you to people you wouldn't otherwise meet, and create experiences you don't expect. All of that will add up to a life well lived—

Your version of a life well lived.

It's different for each of us. The problem is, we spend most of our time thinking about what we're supposed to do and who we're supposed to be for everyone else. We might think other people get what *they* want, but for some reason, *we* can't. We might think pushing our dreams aside is noble or right or just the way the world works.

You can't have what you want, so why bother wanting anything at all?

That way you'll never be disappointed.

Only, it doesn't really work that way, does it?

You're still disappointed; you're just kind of used to it. So what if you're feeling a little stagnant? So what if you're drowning in to-dos and busy all the time? So what if you start putting out fires and taking care of kids and pets and people at work from the second your feet hit the floor in the morning until the moment you collapse in exhaustion every evening?

So what if you're not thriving? You're surviving, aren't you?

But how does that make you feel? (Be honest with yourself for a second; no one else is going to know what you're thinking.) Does it make you feel a little suffocated? Trapped? Stuck? Defeated? Exhausted deep in your soul? Do you ever find yourself wondering what happened to your potential? What happened to that bright-eyed twenty-year-old who was so motivated and had so much energy?

Is that something you want? More motivation and energy?

Great! Add that to the list, because we're here to clarify what you want and create a roadmap to getting it.

And this is not just about your surface feelings. We've got to look at the big picture too. Do you ever have that slightly panicky thought that you might be running out of time?

We all have that thought. Mostly because we are all, technically, running out of time. We only get so much, and anytime we lose someone or there's a health scare, we think about that, but our renewed perspective on life lasts for a short period of time before we fall back into our old habits. Before we go back to putting ourselves way down on the list of priorities.

We'll work on our health after we get through this stressful time at work.

We'll work on our dreams after the kids are out of the house.

We'll make some better (or any) friends later when things aren't so busy.

But how much time do you have?

Think about the number of years you've been alive. How long has that felt? I can tell you my life so far has gone by in a blur. The days are long, but the years are short.

All that putting things off for later? It's got to stop.

Your dreams and desires and talents are there to guide you, not later but NOW.

Pushing yourself down the list of priorities because other people are more important? Nope. That doesn't work either.

It's only in embracing your talents and desires and chasing your dreams and taking care of yourself that you fill your well. That's what gives you joy and energy and enthusiasm, which you can then pass on to others.

You've heard it before, but really think about it... How much better would you be able to take care of others if you took care of yourself a little more?

And where did you get these talents and dreams from in the first place? They were placed in your heart when you were created. How do you think they got there? And what do you want to do with those gifts? Do you want to say, "Gee, I really appreciate the way you gave me this talent and an interest in using it, but instead of working to develop it, I'm going to pass"?

What kind of example is that setting for everyone around you?

And how does it make you feel?

It made me feel terrible. I spent years *knowing* I was ignoring my desires and my dusty old dreams, all the while complaining about my finances and my job and my friends and my lack of hobbies. I flung myself to the floor, rending my garments and crying to the heavens at least once a day. What can I say? You can take the actor off the stage, but you can't take away the drama.

I was stuck in a pit of negativity—of my own making—and I no longer recognized myself. I had become a version of Mel that was so far from who I was meant to be that it felt like wearing the wrong skin. Not only was I hurting myself, I was so miserable that I was hurting everyone I loved.

But I got out of it, and so can you.

Whether you're mired in quicksand or just a little stuck with gum on your shoe, this book is for you.

This is not a book full of answers, because the answers are

different for everyone. This is a book full of questions. The answers are inside you, and we're going to unlock them together.

> You are the only expert on being you.

We're going to figure out what you want. We're going to uncover your dreams and talents. We're going to find your potential. And then I'm going to teach you some strategies you can put into play today to help you become that truer, more authentic, version of you.

We're going to change your life.

It sounds big, and it is, but I'm going to make it easy for you. I'm not going to keep you too long because I know you're busy. This is going to be a fun, quick conversation with someone who loves you, supports you, and just wants to hear all about what matters to you. Think of me like a best friend. I think you're amazing, and I love you so much it literally hurts me to think of you being unhappy and hiding who you really are. I know you've got so much awesome inside you. I can see it, and I want you to see it too.

Oh, and I brought a present for you. You can download your free companion journal at becomingfutureyou.com/book.

You're the hero of this story; I'm just here to guide you on your journey.

Like any good hero, you've been living in the ordinary world for too long—surviving but not thriving. Maybe you've felt the call of your dreams, or maybe you haven't. Maybe they're buried so deep that it will take a push to get you to cross the threshold into adventure. All heroes must eventually go through that doorway; whether they leap through or life gives them a kick in the rear, at some point heroes embark on an epic journey of learning, growing, failing, overcoming, fighting battles, creating relationships, defeating the bad guys, and finally emerging triumphant… and changed. No hero finishes the journey the same as they were when they started.

You've been changing your whole life. You're not the same person now that you were twenty years ago, and the person you are now is not the person you'll be twenty years from now. You're constantly becoming Future You, but I'm going to teach you to do it on purpose and with purpose.

We're going to clarify what you want and who you want to be so you can become the most authentic, truest, 5-star version of Future You.

> This is a battle of life and death. Your life.

This is your one shot at living a meaningful life, at fulfilling your purpose, at using your talents, at living up to your potential. You're not going to be perfect, but you are going to try your best, and that's all anyone can ask.

Your dreams and desires are here to be guideposts on the journey, and I'm here to push you through the doorway. You're not going to wait for life to push you. You're not going to wait for a terminal diagnosis; you're going to leap through, knowing I've got you.

This is your moment. I know it because you wouldn't have picked up this book if you weren't searching, if there wasn't a thought, even buried deep in your subconscious, that said there was room for improvement.

This book is your call to adventure. You're as ready as you're ever going to be.

Let's do this!

DID YOU GET THAT? CHAPTER RECAP:

- The first step to being the hero of your own story is to stop worrying so much about what you're "supposed" to do and start thinking more about what your heart desires.
- It's in embracing your talents and pursuing your dreams that you fill your well and generate energy and enthusiasm that you can pass along to others. Chasing your dreams makes you a nicer person.
- Ignoring your potential for years on end and waiting for "later" will leave you feeling stuck, miserable, and unfulfilled.
- You might already have a vision for your future, or you might not be there yet. Either way, we're going to clarify what you want so you can become the most authentic version of Future You.

Your dreams are yours for a reason, and you are meant to chase them—not later but NOW. Doing so will lead you down the path of a meaningful life.

LET ME ASK YOU THIS:

1. What can you think of right now that you would categorize as one of Present You's dreams? This kind of list is best made as a rapid-fire freewrite. Go to the Chapter 1 section of the journal and use the space provided. Set a timer for five minutes. Write without lifting your pen from the paper until the timer goes

off. The timer forces you to dig deeper and go longer than you normally would, and avoiding pauses in your writing keeps you from overthinking things.
2. What are some of Past You's dreams that you might have given up on or put on hold for later? Set the timer again and answer this one.
3. What's at stake here? Why is it a MUST that you course correct or get your life on your version of the right track? Your answer to this is important; we're tapping into your motivation here!

TAKE ACTION:

1. If you haven't done so already, download the free companion journal at becomingfutureyou.com/book. You can use the space provided to answer these questions, plus I threw in some additional questions for you.
2. It's important to actually write down your answers as opposed to just thinking about them. Writing forces you to define your thoughts and turn them into sentences instead of just random fragments flitting around your brain. Trust me, you're going to get so much more out of this book if you write down your answers.
3. I know you may want to skip ahead and come back to these questions later. That's fine! That's actually why I made the journal: so you can have more flexibility in how and when you do these exercises.

CHAPTER 2: WHO ARE YOU BECOMING?

When I was in high school, one of my teachers approached me about attending leadership camp over the summer. It was a two-week intensive program to be held at one of the best colleges in the state. Every high school was allowed to send two kids, and my school wanted to send me.

I passed.

"I'm not a leader," I said.

Past Mel wanted nothing to do with leadership. Present Mel prides herself on it. I enjoy being a leader in my corner of the freelance industry, I thrive when I'm leading a team of volunteers to run an amazing conference every year, and I love leading my coaching clients and Unlock Your 5-Star Future students.

Being a leader is a huge part of my identity *NOW* because I'm a different person now than I was twenty years ago. And so are you.

PAST, PRESENT, AND FUTURE YOU ARE DIFFERENT CHARACTERS IN THE STORY OF YOUR LIFE

Past You created your current reality, and Present You is creating the reality of Future You. And none of those versions of you are the same.

Are you the same person now that you were five years ago? How about fifteen years ago? Or twenty-five? Or fifty?

We fall into this trap of thinking we're static. We go through childhood and puberty and hit twentyish years old, and that's it. We are who we are, and that's that. (Hello, fixed mindset.)

And as long as we don't look too closely at it, we get to use "the truth about who we are" to avoid doing things we don't want to do:

"I can't run. I have bad knees."

"I'm always late. I'll be late to my own funeral."

"I'm not good at math; I just can't do numbers."

Static. Unchanging. Unable to grow or learn or evolve.

Think back to when you were eighteen years old. What were your interests? What did you do for fun? What were your ambitions? How good of a friend were you back then?

What kind of decision-making skills did you have at eighteen years old?

Did Past You make some important choices that she thought were SO GOOD, and now you're wondering what was going through her head? Did she think being a lawyer was going to be awesome, and now you're wondering why she thought you would be the kind of person who enjoys working a billion hours a week and never sleeping?

If eighteen-year-old you were suddenly zapped into your present life, how well would she handle it?

Not well. *Because she's not you.*

You are a different person now than you were in the past. Things happened, and how you responded changed you. Big things, small things, it all counts. You've been walking around this planet for however long you've been alive, and each day you've become a slightly different person.

You got married.

You had kids.

You lost someone.

You chose a career.

You got divorced.

You won a bunch of money.

You moved across the country or to a different country.

You got bitten by a radioactive spider and developed superhuman abilities.

You developed skills, made choices, responded to chaos. You became a wife, mom, widow, millionaire, Midwesterner, doctor, grocer, baker, candlestick maker. You became Spiderman. You became Present You.

And when you did, Past You disappeared. You are not the same person now that you were any amount of time ago.

I know it's not news to you that your choices have had an impact on your life and shaped who you've become. However, it's not just the big choices that have made a difference; the little choices have had just as much of an impact. I'm talking about your habits.

Not so long ago, I was in the habit of having a brownie after dinner every night. What kind of impact do you think that had on the version of Future Mel I became? If you're guessing that version of Future Mel had a different pants size, you're correct.

Whether or not you have an exercise habit will influence whether or not Future You is in shape. Whether or not you have a tooth-brushing habit will impact whether or not Future You has real teeth. Whether or not you have three-hour-a-day TV habit will affect whether Future You ever achieves your dream of decluttering your house.

Habits may seem like negligible daily actions, but they add up to consequences just as significant as anything else.

Your habits and choices and routine change you.

This is great news because it tells us something important…

FUTURE YOU WILL BE A DIFFERENT PERSON THAN YOU ARE TODAY

You're constantly changing and growing and learning and aging and becoming Future You with every day whether you like it or not.

With this new truth, you can choose to live proactively and become Future You on purpose.

You can choose to get clarity on your goals and dreams and desires. You can choose to discern your special talents. You can choose to act on those things, make progress towards your goals, and use your gifts to positively impact others.

Or you can choose to ignore everything and let life continue to be something that happens *to* you.

The bottom line here is—it all comes down to you.

> You are the hero of this story.

You're in charge of your life. This is *your* hero's journey, and it doesn't belong to anyone else.

Yes, I am aware things happen that are outside your control. But do you know what is always within your control? Your response. Stephen Covey, the author of *The 7 Habits of Highly Effective People*, says, "Look at the word *responsibility*—'response-ability'—the ability to choose your response. Highly proactive people recognize that responsibility. They do not blame circumstances, conditions, or conditioning for their behavior."

You have a responsibility to choose to become the most authentic version of Future You possible. Notice I said the "most authentic" version of you, not the "best." This is not a stronger, better, faster book. This is a "what's right for you?" book.

I'm asking you to become the 5-Star version of yourself. That means the version that's truest to who you are in your soul. I'm asking you to become the version of you who embraces her talents and examines her potential and then works to live up to it. I'm asking you to celebrate your dreams and desires instead of squashing them; those dreams are part of who you are and are meant to serve as guideposts on your hero's journey of becoming 5-Star Future You.

BECOMING AUTHENTIC YOU

We can be victims of the idea that becoming "the best" or "living your best life" always means MORE, MORE, MORE! The answer is always more money, more exercise, a bigger house, more vacations!

But that can't possibly be true for everyone, can it?

Maybe you need to live more simply or more extravagantly. Maybe you need to exercise less and spend more time with your family, or maybe you need to take a break from your family and go to the gym.

I dream of teaching an arena full of people this very concept. I love being on stage. It's when I feel the most alive and like I'm fulfilling my purpose. But I know for most people, getting on a stage with ten thousand people staring at them would be a living nightmare.

Your answers to "what are your dreams?" and "when do you feel most alive?" are going to be different from mine. They'll be different from your neighbor, sister, cousin, partner, and best friend.

You are the expert on being you.

That's why, throughout this book, I'll be asking you questions and counting on you to answer honestly.

In one area of your life, you might find that you're already on the right path. Yay! In discovering that, you'll be able to increase your efforts and work more purposefully towards a clear vision of Future You. In another area, you might find you didn't have much clarity on what you wanted and you've been slowly, but surely, moving further away from who you want to become. And with that knowledge, you'll be able to change course and move forward in a more desirable direction. Also yay!

But why bother doing this work? Why not settle for good enough? Shouldn't we be happy with where we are?

Becoming Future You is not about being dissatisfied with your life and wishing it were different. It's about listening to your gut, embracing who you truly are, and striving to become that version of yourself with joy and gratitude.

> You can be grateful for where you are and still see your potential.

I get all excited and hopeful when I think about Future Mel, but I'm also grateful for where I am; I've come a long way in the past ten years.

Becoming Future You is about enjoying the growth journey and making it like an epic road trip with sightseeing destinations (your dreams!) and a map (strategy!).

Plus growing feels good.

Have you ever gone through a period where you got physically stronger? You started an exercise habit, and walking a mile felt so far and your legs got so sore, but then after a while, you were able to increase your distance to two miles? And you could go faster without getting so out of breath?

You got stronger.

How did that feel? Did you feel pleasure at noting your progress? Were you grateful Past You had stuck with it long enough to make that progress?

YOUR DREAMS ARE YOURS FOR A REASON

Embracing and working towards achieving your potential is not greedy. It's the opposite.

Your dreams are uniquely yours; no one else alive has the exact same dreams and vision and talents and personality and experience as you. And no one can pull it off quite like you.

When one person has a dream, it's because someone else needs to be on the receiving end of that dream. A person has a desire to write a book because someone else needs to read that book. How many times have you been saved by a book? How many times have you been in a difficult season in your life and used fiction to escape? Or binge-watched a TV show on Netflix?

What if the person who wrote that book or TV show never followed their dream to be a writer?

What if no one followed their "impossible" dreams?

Think about all we wouldn't have... movies, comic books, cars, rocket ships, cell phones, foaming hand soap, and tiny robots that clean our houses.

All those things were impossible at some point in time, but then someone had a dream and turned the impossible into reality.

You've got dreams too. Why can't yours come true?

They can.

The pursuit of your dreams, even if they don't turn out exactly as you imagined, will lead you on a journey. You'll learn things about yourself, pick up new skills, have unforgettable experiences, and meet people you never would have met otherwise. Your dreams will guide you down the path of living a meaningful life.

And at the end of the day, it all comes down to one thing: meaning.

Visualize this:

You find yourself standing outside a small building. You don't know how you got there, but you hear voices coming from inside, so you walk through the double doors. You enter a large room and find all the people you know and love. They're all facing forward, listening to someone talk. You look down the long aisle and see your favorite person standing at a podium, addressing everyone. As you get closer to the front, you see a casket. This is a funeral. You start to wonder which of your loved ones has passed when your eyes fall upon a large picture in a frame. It's you. This is your funeral. You look back to the podium, and the words your favorite person is saying finally begin to filter into your brain.

Who is that person, and what are they saying?

The first time I did this "envision your funeral" exercise, what I discovered was that most of the people in my everyday life didn't know me at all. Most of the people I'd pictured being in that room didn't know that I liked to sing or that I'd wanted to be an actor or that I wanted to write a book. I'd gotten so far away from embracing my talents and dreams and who I really was that most of the people who knew me had no idea what my passions were or what I cared about. I think, if pressed, most of them would have said I was a bit argumentative and negative.

What about for you? If you left this world today, what would people say about you?

THE MEANING OF LIFE

Now flash forward for a second to 5-Star Future You. She's in her final days of life, surrounded by her family and friends. She has the calm peace of knowing she has done her best. She followed her dreams and embraced her talents, and even though there were lots of things she never saw coming, she has no regrets. She's fully satisfied with how she lived her life, and she's ready for what comes next.

That could be your reality.

The stakes here are literally life and death.

You don't have to wait for a near-death experience to start living like you're going to die.

You can project forward to end-of-life Future You and ask yourself the questions now: Was my life meaningful? Did I make a difference? Will anyone care that I'm gone?

When I work with my coaching clients, we inevitably get to a place where, in answering one of my questions, they come back with the answer: "Because that's the meaning of life."

The only thing is, every one of them has *a different definition of the meaning of life*.

Just like your dreams, your version of a meaningful life is unique to you.

If you want to live a meaningful life, you've got to define what that means for YOU.

That's what we're going to do in this book; by the end, you're going to have a clearer answer than you have now. And it's going to be YOUR unique answer. Every single person who reads this book will come up with something different.

Maybe you've already done a little work around this idea of becoming Future You. That's great! Let's make sure you're working efficiently and with intention.

Or maybe you've got no idea what the 5-star version of your life would even look like. That's okay too. We'll figure it out together.

Either way, it's going to take work.

FUTURE YOU IS NOT JUST GOING TO SHOW UP

Sometimes we create a vision of our Future Selves who is less stressed and more organized and has her act together… and then we continue to do the same things we've always done and wonder why she hasn't shown up yet.

Future You is not your mom. She's not just going to show up and fix your mess.

You've got to fix it yourself, and in fixing it, you become the kind of person who doesn't have a mess.

You want to be an author? No one can hand you a finished book and say, "Poof! You're an author!" It's in writing the book that you become the kind of person who has written a book.

It's in training for the marathon that you become the kind of person who has run a marathon.

It's in decluttering your house that you become the kind of person who doesn't have a cluttered house.

It's in pursuing your dreams that you become the kind of person who has achieved them. Future You is not going to just show up; you have to do the work of becoming her.

IT'S ACTUALLY LESS WORK THAN YOU'RE DOING NOW

Thinking this sounds like a lot of work? It is, but you're already working hard. This is not going to be *more* work than you're already doing; it's going to be *more focused* work. You're going to become more intentional about your efforts and your energy, which will result in your feeling better, not worse.

Think about the difficult things you've overcome in the past…

The time you set a goal that seemed too far out of reach, but you accomplished it.

The time that person did that terrible thing to you, but you survived.

The time life threw you a heartbreaking curveball, but you learned so much and you're stronger for it.

As my friend Tawdra says, "So far, you have a 100 percent survival rating."

Those things didn't kill you, and as a result, you're tough as steel. You could basically bench-press a pickup truck at this point. You can absolutely do something as simple as reimagining your life and taking small but impactful actions to become that version of you.

That means the choice is yours. Are you going to become Future You on purpose?

Are you going to choose to be the hero of your story?

Or are you going to use the excuse that you're not in control and continue to let life be something that just happens to you?

No matter what you decide in this moment, you are still becoming Future You. The question is… are you going to like the results?

Becoming Future You on purpose is going to take work. It's going to take vision. It's going to take reading this book and answering my questions honestly. It might not be easy, but it will be exciting, and we're going to do it together.

DID YOU GET THAT? CHAPTER RECAP:

- You are not the same person now that you were ten years ago. Things happened, you made choices, you developed habits, and you became a different version of you.
- This is great news because it means Future You will be a different person than you are today. Now that you know that, you can choose to live proactively and become Future You on purpose.
- Becoming Future You isn't about being dissatisfied with your life; it's about embracing your potential and striving to become the most authentic version of you on purpose.
- When you pursue your dreams, you define and create your version of a meaningful life as well as help out the people who need to be on the receiving end of your dreams. (Want to start a podcast? You have that dream because someone out there needs to hear it!)
- Whether you know a lot or a little about what you want for Future You, we're going to work together to define your version of a meaningful life so you can start living it now.

LET ME ASK YOU THIS:

1. What are some of the positive ways Present You is different from Past You? What have you learned? How have you grown? How are you wiser now than you were in the past?
2. What did you think about when you envisioned your funeral? Who was talking? What were they saying? If you left this world today, what would people say

about you? And how is that different from what you would like them to remember?

3. You're stronger than you think. What are some of the challenges Past You has already overcome? Make a list.
4. What habits do you currently have that you suspect are not creating the version of Future You you'd like to become? (Like Past Mel's daily brownie habit.)
5. What do you already know to be true about Future You? Set a timer for five minutes, start writing, and don't pause until the timer goes off. Just hurl out all the random things you can think of… Maybe you know Future You has more time or is less stressed. Don't worry about the how or the why; this is just your first step in defining Future You.

CHAPTER 3: IT'S NOT ABOUT YOU

"Whenever someone gives you a compliment, you look like you're in actual physical pain."

What?

My best friend Jackie and I were fixing our favorite college meal, off-brand macaroni and cheese, when she dropped this bomb on me.

"It's like you can't brush it off fast enough," she said.

Jackie and I were the kind of college friends who lived together, scheduled our classes together, and ate most meals together. We talked about *everything*—from the ridiculous thing one of our fellow acting students had done to the meaning of life and the depths of the Universe. We developed a bunch of psychological theories over the years that, once I finally took the mandatory psych class in my senior year, turned out to be real phenomena with far less interesting names than the ones we'd invented.

"You always argue with people when they say something nice about you," Jackie said.

She was right, of course, but it took me years to agree with her and even longer to figure out why that was true.

For as long as I could remember, I thought it was morally wrong to feel proud of myself, to note my accomplishments, or to strengthen my skills. I thought being good at things meant I was showing off, and showing off was unequivocally wrong.

There were adults who kept telling me I needed to be humbler, and I was pretty sure they meant "Mel, don't let people see your talents. It makes them feel bad about themselves."

So I began putting my acting skills to good use and became a chameleon. Even though I knew I was good at communicating and had an excellent vocabulary, I'd dumb down my language so I wouldn't make other people feel bad about not knowing the word I was using. Sometimes I pretended I didn't know the answer in class so someone else could answer the teacher. Occasionally, I'd purposefully misspell something in my homework. You know, so the teacher could feel good about finding my mistake. After all, I felt so good about catching their mistakes.

It was all part of my grand plan to keep people from thinking I was showing off.

THERE'S NOTHING ENLIGHTENED ABOUT SHRINKING

What I didn't realize at the time was not only was I taking my talents and burying them, I was also robbing myself of the things that made me feel best: growing, making progress, and words of affirmation.

I continued this way into my thirties. And I continued to feel worse and worse about myself. This "dumb it down" strategy was sucking the joy right out of my life, but it took reading a quote by Marianne Williamson to challenge my beliefs. She said:

"We ask ourselves, 'Who am I to be brilliant, gorgeous, talented, fabulous?' Actually, who are you not to be? You are a child of God. Your playing small does not serve the world. ***There is nothing enlightened about shrinking so that other people won't feel insecure around you.***"

— Marianne Williamson, *A Return to Love: Reflections on the Principles of "A Course in Miracles"* (emphasis mine)

My shrinking was not only hurting myself, but it was also hurting others. I'd spent my whole life trying to do what was "right" and putting others first, only to discover that withholding my talents was doing the very thing I was trying to avoid.

In the last chapter, I was all "you're the hero" and "it's all about you." How did that make you feel? Strong? Empowered? Significant? Loved?

Or gross?

If you're thinking you shouldn't be the hero, that the hero should actually be your kids, your spouse, your sister, your neighbor, your church, your hairstylist, *anybody* but you, you're not alone.

Some of us fall into this trap of feeling guilty or selfish or any number of negative emotions when we turn our attention inward. We think it's fundamentally wrong to focus on ourselves. We think that in putting attention on ourselves, we're stealing it from the people and things we're "supposed" to pay attention to. (Hello, mom guilt.)

If this sounds like you, you probably got this message sometime in childhood, just like I did. Tiny Past You picked up the idea from your teachers, your parents, your aunts, uncles, cousins, the TV shows you watched, the books you read, or any number of places. Tiny Past You internalized some sort of message saying it was selfish or sinful or disgustingly self-centered to focus on yourself. It was wrong, and you were wrong for doing it.

If you're feeling icky at this moment, chances are we just activated some sort of messaging from your childhood that says, "No way, babe! Everything isn't about you."

It's okay to accept compliments. It's okay to invest in your interests and hone your talents. It's okay to let your light shine. When you turn your focus inward, you not only bring joy to yourself, you set a great example for others around you.

SOMEONE IS PAYING ATTENTION TO YOU

Is it selfish to drink water? Should you actually be saving all the water for your family? Or is there enough to go around? As a matter of fact, have you ever drunk a glass of water in front of your kids just to prove to them it actually isn't disgusting and, yes, they can drink their own glass of water, thank you very much?

What about when you go to the gym after work? Are you setting an example for your spouse? Logically, we can say that this is probably true, and research backs up our conclusion.

A 2014 study by researchers at University College London followed 3,700 couples over a period of twelve years and discovered that "men and women are more likely to make a positive health behavior change if their partner does too." The participating couples answered questionnaires every four years, and across all domains surveyed (smoking, physical activity, and weight loss), the researchers found that when one partner adopted a new healthy behavior, the other partner was more likely to make a positive change.[1]

You're having an influence all day every day—on your kids, your spouse, your community, the barista at the coffee shop, the guy you've never talked to but who walks his dog at the same time you do. You do not live in a bubble. No matter what you think about your level of importance in the world, let me assure you, you are having an impact.

When you use your talents, you're setting one kind of example. When you bury them, you're setting another. Someone is always watching and learning what to do from you.

When those around you see that investing in yourself makes you happier, more joyful, and kinder to others, you have an opportunity to lead by example.

CARING FOR YOURSELF *IS* CARING FOR OTHERS

Growth is a basic human need, just like the water you drank in front of your kids. Just like the shelter you insist on having and the love you crave. Like every living thing, you are designed to grow.

Flowers grow.

Puppies grow.

The mold in the container of leftover lasagna you keep forgetting to throw out grows.

Growth is natural. When you grow on purpose, you're living in alignment with your natural design. When you fight that growth and refuse to embrace your talents and bat away opportunities for self-care and staunchly resist trying anything you don't already know how to do, you're not only fighting the natural order of things, you're being incredibly selfish.

Think about it. When you've had a great night's sleep, are you nicer to everyone the next day?

When you're excited about working on that blanket you're learning to crochet, are you in a better mood?

When you get a chance to do yoga after work instead of rushing straight home and starting dinner, are you more patient with your pets?

Yes, of course you are.

When you take care of yourself, you're better able to care for others. We all know this. The problem is that we downgrade what "care for yourself" means. We put the basics in there: shelter, water, food (but not healthy food; that's a luxury). And then we shirk on all our other needs like sleep, money, time to recharge, exercise, and growth.

Want to care for others? You've got to take care of you first.

SOMEONE NEEDS YOU TO BE FUTURE YOU

Someone needs to be on the receiving end of your talents. Someone needs to be on the receiving end of that dream you feel called (but are afraid) to chase. Someone needs you to become that more authentic version of you so you can fill a gap in their life.

That book you secretly want to write… Someone needs to read that book.

That job you're scared to apply for... That company needs you.

That speaking gig you're scared to book... Someone needs to hear your words.

That solo at church you're afraid to audition for... Someone needs to hear your voice.

Someone is out there, waiting for you to use your gifts. Kind of puts things in perspective, doesn't it? When you hide your talents and put off your dreams, it's not just you you're hurting.

BEING THE HERO MEANS HELPING YOURSELF *SO THAT* YOU CAN HELP OTHERS

The best way to be of service to others is to embrace what makes you YOU.

- When you become the more authentic, 5-star version of you, you will be a more pleasant human to everyone who interacts with you.
- When you use your talents, you'll positively impact everyone on the receiving end.
- When you chase your dreams, you set a positive example for everyone who sees you doing it.
- When you achieve your dreams, the journey you went on to get there impacts an untold number of people.
- When you follow your desires, you stop sitting in someone else's seat. (That job you don't like but you're forcing yourself to do? Someone else might LOVE being in that role, but they can't step into it because you're there.)

The Universe is like a giant puzzle. Every piece is needed to create the whole picture. When you listen to your desires and embrace your talents, you take your place in the Universe.

> Taking care of yourself, embracing your talents, and growing into Future You on purpose is one of the most selfless things you can possibly do.

When you accept your hero's journey, it's not just for you but for everyone else around you. It's only in making yourself a priority that you're able to selflessly help others. Putting this off, continuing to wallow in the muck, continuing to ignore your talents, continuing to be poor if you know you're meant to be rich—that's all selfish.

Someone is waiting for you to do your thing. What are you going to do about it?

DID YOU GET THAT? CHAPTER RECAP:

- There's nothing enlightened about shrinking and hiding your talents. You serve others best when you let your light shine.
- If you're feeling gross about putting so much focus on yourself, you're not alone! You probably picked up some not-so-helpful beliefs in your childhood that are telling you focusing on yourself is selfish.
- The truth is, when you turn your attention inward and allow yourself to grow, you live in alignment with nature, set a great example for those around you, and become a kinder, happier person.
- Simply by working towards your dreams, you will have a positive impact on the people around you. People you know and some you don't will benefit from you becoming 5-Star Future You!

LET ME ASK YOU THIS:

1. What's everything you can remember being told about being "selfish?" Or what are some of the examples you've observed about what qualifies as selfish or not? Do you actually consider those things selfish? Or is that someone else's voice in your head?
2. Who are you taking care of? Make a list of all the people, plants, and animals you help on a regular basis. I mean everyone from the friend at work whose coffee you always grab to the kid at home whose mouth (and other parts) you always wipe. I bet you're doing a lot more than you're giving yourself credit for.
3. Now, look back at that list and ask yourself, "Who would benefit from me feeling more peaceful, joyful, fulfilled, rested, or happier?" (Is it everyone? I bet it's everyone.) But seriously, how would each of the people on that list benefit if you took a bit more time to care for yourself? Which interactions might be improved? When specifically might you be more loving or patient?
4. Pick one dream or goal (even if it's a tiny goal that you don't think counts as a dream!) and answer these questions:
5. Who might benefit while I'm working towards this goal?
6. How will working towards this goal make me different to be around?
7. Who might be on the receiving end of this dream and would benefit from me achieving it?

---

1. Jackson SE, Steptoe A, Wardle J. "The Influence of Partner's Behavior on Health Behavior Change: The English Longitudinal Study of Ageing,"

JAMA Intern Med. 2015;175(3):385–392. doi:10.1001/jamainternmed.2014.7554

https://jamanetwork.com/journals/jamainternalmedicine/fullarticle/2091401

CHAPTER 4: THE JOURNEY IS THE POINT

When I was ten years old, I only wanted one thing for my future… to be Garth Brooks. Not just a singer or a star, but Garth Brooks specifically. I liked the way he entertained thousands of people at a time, his exaggerated facial expressions, and the cool microphone he wore. No standing in front of a stationary mic for this guy. He had a microphone Strapped. To. His. Face. That's commitment to showmanship.

That desire to be on stage followed me all the way to high school where, after being in a few plays, I decided musical theatre was the track for me. I applied to attend a college with one of the best theatre programs in our state and couldn't wait to start my freshman year.

Within a couple of months, I realized I'd made a mistake. I wasn't allowed to be in any plays as a freshman, so without the high of getting on stage, I just had the constant criticism of training to be an actor.

By the time I finished my degree, I wanted nothing to do with acting.

YOUR DREAMS ARE DOORWAYS TO NEW EXPERIENCES

Do I regret getting the degree or following my dream? Nope. If I hadn't had the burning desire to be trained as an actor, I wouldn't have picked that college. And if I hadn't picked that college, I wouldn't have met my best friend, Jackie. And if I hadn't met Jackie, I wouldn't have had all those conversations about how brains work. And if I hadn't had those conversations, I wouldn't be writing this book.

So I suffered through theatre school for you. You're welcome.

Just kidding. I'm grateful for my degree, and I use it in many ways every day.

I haven't yet achieved my dream of standing on a stage in front of thousands while wearing a wireless headset, but there's still time. And chasing that dream sent me on a journey that shaped the trajectory of my life. I met people, I learned things, and I had experiences that I wouldn't have had without that dream.

> Your dreams are there to guide you on the journey, and the journey is the point.

YOUR DREAMS REQUIRE ACTION

Your unique and scary dreams are yours for a reason. They are meant to push, pull, and cajole you into taking the steps you must to create your version of a meaningful life.

You can't think your way into achieving a dream. You must take action. And that action leads you down a path of discovery.

When you chase your dream of becoming a turnip farmer, you might meet other turnip farmers and find some of the best friends you've ever had. You might realize the injustices that exist in the turnip-farming industry and work with your new friends to create better practices and a healthier environment. Once you achieve your dream of setting up your roadside turnip stand, you might find that the interaction of talking to strangers is exactly what you were craving, and that might lead you to your next big dream to move to the coast and become a carriage tour guide.

It's not about achieving the dream; it's about who you become while you're pursuing the dream.

YOUR DREAMS REQUIRE CLARITY

You won't know the twists and turns of the road ahead, but you've got to know which mountain you're driving towards. You've got to define what you want so your dreams can serve as guideposts on the road ahead.

The roadmap of a meaningful life comes not from what you're supposed to do but what you dream about doing.

Throughout this book, we're going to work on designing 5-Star Future You. Who is she? What does she do for fun? What kind of people does she have in her life? What has she achieved?

We're going to work on this so you can gain clarity on your dreams, embark on your journey, and make more informed and strategic choices going forward.

We're going to unleash your dreams and desires and bring them into the light, which can be exciting and scary. If you're starting to feel a bit nervous, good! That means you're taking this seriously.

THE JOURNEY IS BETTER WITH FRIENDS

This kind of activity is even more exhilarating if someone else is doing it with you. Do you know someone else who needs to turn their attention inward? Someone who deserves more love and care from themselves? Someone who will keep you moving forward and hold you accountable even if the road ahead is difficult? Invite them to start reading this book at the same time so that you can talk about your epic plans for Future You. And while you're at it, both of you can join our Facebook group. The link to join is in your journal, which you can download at becomingfutureyou.com/book.

THE ONLY WRONG MOVE IS NOT MOVING

I know I've been telling you that all your choices matter, but let's take some pressure off here. There are no wrong moves. The only wrong decision is trying to stand still.

You can learn something from any decision you make even if you get down the road and realize you're not where you want to be. I could look back at eighteen-year-old Past Mel's decision to be an actor and think, "What an idiot. She sure messed up." But instead, I choose to focus on what I learned and what I gained while still altering my path going forward.

Just because twenty-year-old Past You decided you should be a pediatrician doesn't mean you still have to be a doctor. There's more than one way to pay off student loans.

> You don't have to wait for retirement to reinvent yourself.

Past You was doing the best she could with the information she had at the time. And don't forget, just like Present You, there were lots of things that happened that she couldn't control. Present You knows more about yourself and the world. After you finish this book, you'll know more about what you want for Future You. Armed with that information, you can make different choices going forward.

No matter what kind of crazy decisions Past You made, you are still here. You survived.

Take the pressure off Present You. Yes, we're working to become Future You with more intention, but don't let yourself be paralyzed with indecision, thinking that you can only make "right" choices going forward. There's no such thing, and you learn more from failure than you do from success.

You will make mistakes. When you do, get up, brush yourself off, and go forward armed with new knowledge and life experience. What do you think makes our elders so wise? They've. Been. Through. It.

IF YOU'RE WAITING TO BE READY, YOU'LL NEVER BE.

The journey is what makes you ready.

Writing the book is what makes you capable of writing the book, not thinking about it or taking classes. Sure, instruction is helpful, but getting a degree in creative writing doesn't automatically turn you into a writer. Writing the book is what turns you into the kind of person who has a finished book.

Exercise is what gets you in shape, not thinking about exercising or buying workout clothes or joining a gym. Doing the work is what causes your muscles to firm and your heart to strengthen. It's only in building up your endurance by going on run after run that you become the kind of person who runs a 5k.

YOU ARE READY TO CROSS THE THRESHOLD

You might not feel ready, but I know that you are. You wouldn't still be with me if you didn't feel the pull to change, the call to do something different, the desire to be more intentional with what's left of your life.

And now you have knowledge you can never erase:

You are becoming Future You with every choice and every action.

And now that you know that, things can be so much better.

The thing about being called to adventure is that answering the call requires not just listening to the Universe but making a decision—a real decision from which there is no turning back.

And that's when we get scared.

There are many times in our lives that we feel the call, and then we refuse. We know we need to change, but we ignore our gut. We know we're in the wrong situation, but we suck it up and keep going. We know we're killing ourselves with our schedule, but we just put our heads down and try to get through.

We refuse the call. It's scary, and we'd rather stick with our current level of discomfort. We wait for something to happen.

We wait for a terminal diagnosis, either for ourselves or someone else. We wait to lose our job or our home or someone important. We wait to have the rug yanked out from under us.

You don't have to hit rock bottom to make a change.

Maybe you've previously refused to make a decision because it felt like a betrayal of Past You. She made all those choices and got you where you are today. Changing your mind can feel like admitting you were wrong, but take a deep breath and ask yourself:

Would you prefer to continue living the wrong life just to prove a point to yourself?

Or would you rather be the YOU you're meant to be and lead a more satisfying, joyful, meaningful life with the time you've got left?

For me, the decision came when I realized I couldn't stand another day of looking in the mirror and disliking myself. I'd been on a downward trajectory for years—becoming more and more negative, gossipy, and convinced my life was pointless. I knew I wasn't living up to my potential, and I felt terrible about it. And I'd felt terrible about it for *years*.

I kept waiting for something outside myself to change. And then I got tired of waiting.

On December 30, 2014, I made a no-turning-back decision to become a more positive version of myself, to dig myself out of the pit I'd created, to find the real Mel again. I committed to becoming Positive Future Mel.

And then I spent the next day sobbing.

My husband and I were on a road trip, and there's nothing like being locked in a car for twelve hours straight to give you plenty of time to reflect. I was grieving. I didn't comprehend it at the time, but I had made a real decision to kill off Past Mel so a better, brighter Future Mel could grow in her place. And I needed to mourn Past Mel before moving on.

Just like losing someone, it was disorienting, heart-wrenching, and terrifying.

But it was a real decision, and I never looked back. By January 1, I was ready to take my first uncertain step forward. I didn't know what I was doing, but I knew I wasn't going back. I couldn't be more grateful that I made that choice because it turned me into who I am today… someone I enjoy being!

NOW IT'S YOUR TURN

Are you going to step through a doorway of no return? Are you going to step firmly, if uncertainly, into your new life? Or are you going to try to maintain an impossible status quo?

You don't have to have any answers at this point. All I'm asking is that you commit to moving forward, to visualizing the most authentic version of you even if it makes you feel feelings you don't like, and to be willing to make changes. I'm asking you to decide to become Future You on purpose.

You might be on shaky ground, but I've got you.

Don't put this decision off until later. You and I both know "later" almost never comes. Or maybe you've put this decision off previously and now *this* is later! You don't have to have all the answers or even any answers yet. All you have to do is decide to become that authentic version of you and let me guide you through the next steps.

5-Star Future You is waiting for us to take action. You as the hero, me as your guide.

DID YOU GET THAT? CHAPTER RECAP:

- Your dreams are not destinations to be achieved or not, but guideposts on the journey of a meaningful life.
- This is a huge relief because it means if you decide you no longer want a particular dream, those years of chasing it were not wasted. You met people and had experiences and learned things you wouldn't have otherwise.
- You don't need to wait until you know everything you want for Future You to take your first step in the right direction.
- Creating your vision for Future You is going to come from answering my questions and taking action. The farther you get down the road, the more you'll know about who you want to become.
- Any road trip is better with friends, and this is no different. Invite some of your friends to start reading this book so you can all chat about your discoveries. If you'd like to read this with your book club, let me know and I'll Zoom in for a virtual chat.
- Don't put too much pressure on yourself to wait until you know the "right" next step. You're just going to do your best, and even "wrong" moves can offer a great opportunity to learn and grow.
- Even if you don't think you're ready, you are. There's no need to wait until later—just keep reading this book, and I'll guide you through the next steps to becoming a more authentic version of you.

LET ME ASK YOU THIS:

1. Can you think of any times in your life when you've given up on a dream and it was absolutely the right decision? What did you learn from pursuing that dream even though you didn't see it to completion?
2. Are there any dreams you've put on the back burner because they're too hard or you're not sure how you'll achieve them? What are they?
3. If you kill off the old version of you to make room for the more authentic version, what are you afraid will happen?

ACT II: VISION IS CREATED

CHAPTER 5: THE ENEMIES CLOSE IN

WHEN MY BABCIA WAS A KID, she got out of bed one morning and fell down. She told her mom that her legs didn't feel right and that she was having trouble lifting her arm high enough to turn on the light.

"You're fine," my great-grandmother told her.

The next day, my babcia tried to get out of bed and fell again.

"Get up," my great-grandmother said.

Day after day, the same thing kept happening, and my babcia kept getting back up.

Turned out she had polio.

Eventually her mom believed her, and they took her to the doctor, but my babcia insists the reason she can walk today is because she kept getting back up. She kept using those muscles even as the disease was weakening her arms and legs. Her school had a long flight of stairs that she had to climb every morning, and even though she often fell, she got back up as the other kids laughed at her.

She kept getting back up, kept using and strengthening those muscles, and today she can walk.

As soon as you decide to cross the threshold and become 5-Star Future You, something might happen. Something that might seem like a setback or a sign that you made a bad choice and shouldn't continue.

What's actually happening is this:

You just said some version of "I want to be stronger."

Now the Universe is getting to work right away to help you become stronger, which often looks like knocking you down. Remember, you can't just snap your fingers and become a stronger version of yourself. It's only in going through *The Hard Thing* that you become the kind of person who has overcome *The Hard Thing*.

Back in 2014, after I finished bawling my eyes out over my big decision, I told a friend about my plan to become a positive person.

She said: "I don't want you to be a positive person. I want you to be my negative, snarky friend."

Ouch.

Even now it seems shocking. How could someone who professed to care about me say something so terrible?

The answer is simple. She didn't want to lose her friend, and even though I didn't use those exact words, I'd made it clear I was going to kill off old Mel.

At the time, that experience was disorienting. I mean, I'd already decided to become this more authentic version of myself, which was scary enough, but then when I told someone I thought was going to support me, she did the opposite!?

Now I can see that interaction for the gift it was. It made me stronger. It made me double down on my decision. It activated a serious force of motivation for me, which is "don't tell me what to do!"

Whatever the Universe throws at you will be just as customized as my first "setback." It will make you stronger. It will give you the opportunity to shore up your belief in yourself and get clear on why this new adventure matters to you.

One thing is for certain: when you trip over that first obstacle and the enemies close in, you are not going to lie down in the mud. No! You are going to remember "Mel said this was going to happen," and then you are going to be like my babcia and you are going to get back up.

IDENTIFY YOUR TEAM

There are a lot of players in your hero's journey, and it's time to get to know some of them. My friend's harsh words caused me to ask an important question:

Who is on Team Future Me?

Who in my life was going to support me in this venture of becoming the kind of person who didn't gossip or talk junk about her spouse? After my friend said she wanted me to stay snarky and negative, I realized Future Mel's team members might not be the same people with whom I was gossiping and complaining.

Which wiped out most of my close friends.

After you cross through the doorway of no return with your no-nonsense decision, Future You's enemies are going to take action to keep you where you are.

For me, it was my friend batting my precious idea away like a worthless piece of garbage.

The word *enemies* might sound harsh, so let me clarify. We're not talking about vindictive villains who twirl their mustaches and release their alien armies upon the planet. An enemy could be someone who loves you and cares about you but actively wants to hold you back from becoming Future You. Maybe they're like my friend and they don't want to lose what they perceive to be your good qualities. Maybe they love you and they're afraid you're going to get hurt, and so they're trying to keep you safe by talking you out of your dreams. Maybe they just can't see the vision you've created and are worried you don't know what you're doing. Whatever their motivation, the bottom line is the same.

> Enemies don't want you to grow. They prefer you just the way you are: stuck.

Have you heard what happens if you put a bunch of crabs in a bucket? You would think, left to their own devices, the crabs would climb out of the bucket and escape, right? Wrong. If one crab starts to escape, the other crabs pull him back down.

Your enemies are like a bunch of crabs stuck in a bucket with you. For whatever reason, they don't want you to leave the bucket.

You've got to know who is on your side and who isn't. Or rather, who will be on Future You's side. To do this, we've got to create clarity around the kind of people with whom Future You spends time.

When Future You tells her friends about her dream to sell her house and become a goat farmer, will they be supportive? Or will they point out that she can't even keep a houseplant alive; how in the world does she expect to keep a goat alive?

When she tells them she wants to take up belly dancing, will they laugh or will they say, *"Heck yes! Live your best life!"*

When she tells them she wants to open a new restaurant called Mel's Nacho Emporium that specializes in all different kinds of nachos, will they remind her, *"Most restaurants fail in the first year?"* Will they point out that vegans don't eat nachos and refuse to listen when she tries to tell them about cashew cheese? Or will they say, *"Awesome! I've got a friend who has a successful restaurant; you can talk to her."*

DESIGN FUTURE YOU'S FRIENDSHIPS

What kinds of friends does Future You have? This is your moment to simply imagine the kind of people you'd like to have in your life. Instead of thinking about people you already know, try creating imaginary characters. Just like your imaginary friend from childhood, Future You's friends can have any characteristics you want.

What do Future You's friends do for fun? What are their interests? What are their hobbies?

How do they treat their partners?

What's their financial status?

Where do they go on vacation?

Are they parents? What kind of parents are they?

Are they leaders in some capacity? What kind of leaders are they?

What do they do for a living?

What's their spiritual life like? What are their values? Do they value personal growth?

How do they behave as a friend? Do they check in on you? Do they spend time with you? How do they offer support? How do they receive your friendship in return?

What amount of time do they expect to spend with you? How often do you want to see them?

If you haven't already, take a minute and download the FREE companion journal at becomingfutureyou.com/book. I've included these questions for you there.

Let me say it again: you can make up whatever you want for the answers to these questions. Whatever you want! You can imagine that Future You has an entire network of goat-farmer friends who play cards every Friday night if that's something that sounds fun to you. There are no wrong answers here, and even if you're not sure you're hitting on the "right" answers, remember that general ideas are better than nothing at all. What we're doing is clarifying the kind of support system and relationships you'd like to have in the 5-star version of your life.

PRESENT YOU'S ENEMIES AND ALLIES

Now let's return to Present You.

Who in your life meets at least some of these criteria? Who has the values you're looking for in your relationships? Who supports you the way you want to be supported? **Who is already on Team Future You?**

We can be fooled by labels like Best Friend Forever and Girl Tribe. Just because someone had a special label in your life at one point in time doesn't mean they need to stay in that role forever. *Just because she was in your wedding doesn't mean she has to be in your life now.*

A lot of the people I considered friends weren't going to be supportive of my dreams. I wanted to become a positive, joyful person, and hanging out with them and gossiping made me feel like I'd just mainlined an entire bag of BBQ-flavored chips… a little sick to my stomach.

You might have started this chapter already knowing that some people are like poison to your dreams. Or you might be starting to have the niggle of a thought in the back of your brain that says, "I do have a couple of friends/family members who make me feel bad about myself."

I know it's not fun to come to this realization, but identifying who is opposed to you becoming Future You is going to be important as you move forward in this journey. We're working on this vision of who Future You is, and as you get more excited, you're going to want to talk about your goals and dreams and the changes you want to make.

And that will be when you really start to find out who will be on Future You's side.

Maybe you'll have a conversation like this:

YOU: I'm tired of being so tired all the time, and Future Me has way more energy. I'm going to try giving up sugar for a month and see if it makes me feel better.

YOUR FRIEND: Great idea! I've been thinking the same thing. I'll join you.

Yay! Now you've got some evidence that friend is willing to grow with you. Add her to your list of allies.

What you've got to watch out for are conversations that go like this:

YOU: My joints have been killing me. I'm going to give up alcohol for a month and see if that helps.

YOUR FRIEND: Why!? Do you hate yourself?

YOU: No, but my joints hurt.

YOUR FRIEND: I heard drinking a glass of wine a day is good for you. Why would you give up those health benefits?

YOU: It's only a month.

YOUR FRIEND: Suit yourself. I bet you won't last a week.

Wow, your friend sounds like a jerk, right!? Cut her some slack. What's really happening in her mind is something like this:

She's giving up alcohol? Oh no! Who will go to happy hour with me? Maybe I should give it up too. No, that sounds hard. And I don't want to. Whatever. It's fine. She probably won't make it a month anyway.

Her reaction has nothing to do with you. It's all about her and how she needs you to fit into a specific mold. And that tells us she's not one of Future You's allies; at least not at this moment. She might come around, but don't waste your time trying to convince her to change. You need that energy to work on your own changes.

Pay attention to your conversations and start asking the question, "Is this person my ally or my enemy?"

I know what you're thinking… *Mel, isn't there a neutral zone here? Does everyone have to be an enemy or an ally?*

Of course there's a gray area; don't be dramatic. This is a sliding scale. Unlike in the movies, there isn't a clear delineation between "good guys" and "bad guys." But there are also probably *a lot* of people in your life who fall closer to the enemy camp than you've been willing to admit, and those people have been influencing you.

If Future You is different than Present You, then Future You has a different level of friendships.

You've probably heard that you become the average of the five people you spend the most time with, right? This group of people you're letting influence you are controlling who you are becoming.

Past You's friends influenced Present You. Present You's friends are currently influencing Future You.

I'm not telling you to kick people out of your life, but as you start to notice the difference between your enemies and your allies, you can get strategic about protecting Future You.

For those people in your life you already know are leading the enemy camp—those people who put you down, argue with everything you say, want to run your life and tell you what you "should" do next and what you should do after that too—for those people who leave you feeling drained instead of energized, let's talk about some strategies.

STRATEGY #1: BE INTENTIONAL ABOUT WHEN YOU SPEND TIME WITH YOUR ENEMIES

You know those people who leave you feeling exhausted and not so great about yourself after every interaction? Become less available to hanging out with those people. Get slower about replying to their texts or returning their calls.

Purposefully wait a day to get back to them, and when you do, don't apologize for taking so long.

You are constantly training people how to treat you. Train them that you're slow at messaging, and eventually they'll get used to it.

When you do spend time with those enemies, be strategic about when you do it. Need to give a big presentation at work? Don't have dinner with that "friend" the night before. Does gossiping with your group of girlfriends always give you an emotional hangover and have you questioning whether or not you're a good person? Show up late to the Saturday-evening cookout and leave early. Does that friend you made at the gym subtly put you down and say things like: "Wow! Still haven't increased your speed on the treadmill yet? Hmmmm." Change the time you go to the gym so you don't see that person anymore!

I worked with a coaching client who was a caregiver for her elderly parents. It was hard work, and her relationship with her parents was already complicated; her father was always belittling her and making her feel like she wasn't enough. Still, this client decided that Future Her was the kind of person who took care of her aging parents, so she wanted to continue doing it. However, she decided she would change her schedule so she had time to work on her pottery, which brought her joy and made her feel like she was fulfilling her purpose, *before* she went to visit her parents each day.

If someone is draining you, don't spend time with them before doing your difficult or creative work. If they steal your energy and attack your confidence, don't use your best energy for dealing with that person. Use your best energy for becoming Future You and let them have some, but not all, of what's left.

STRATEGY #2: DON'T TELL YOUR ENEMIES YOUR DREAMS

If you know someone is going to try to kill your dreams… Don't Tell Them. Let's say your cat is one of your closest relationships, but you suddenly find out your cat loves to shred paper. With this new knowledge, would you bring her your prized origami collection and place it in front of her for inspection? No!

Your dream is like a tiny bird that hasn't learned to fly yet. Are you going to hold out your hand with your little bird dream and let a friend smack it to the ground? No.

If you know someone is going to be a jerk about your dreams, don't tell them. I'm sure they'll be super supportive after you're already successful. That's fine. They can tell people about how they knew you when.

STRATEGY #3: DON'T LISTEN TO ENEMIES ON THE INTERNET

Once upon a time, I followed an influencer on the internet. I read everything she wrote, watched all her YouTube videos, and followed her on Instagram. I thought, "This chick has it all together, and she's doling out life and career advice like it's miniature candy bars on Halloween. If I just do what she says, I'll achieve the same level of success."

Only her advice wasn't working for me. And it was making me feel bad about myself. And her life wasn't anything like mine. And yet I kept comparing myself to her!

Believe me, I understand the compulsion to check and see what the "successful" people are doing. I mean, if they're putting their secrets out there on the internet, why not read them?

If they're not helping you become Future You, that's why not. If comparing yourself to them is making you feel crappy, stop scrolling.

You are more in control of what you see on the internet than almost any other input in your life. If you don't check the news for a whole day, is someone going to come knock on your apartment door and tell you the eighty-seven horrific things that have happened since you last checked? You literally have to bring some kind of screen into view and look at it. Cutting out enemies on the internet is the easiest kind of upgrade you can make. Here's how you do it:

1. Aggressively unfollow people on social media. If their content makes you feel bad, you do not have to look at it.
2. Turn off notifications on your devices. Why do you need to know immediately if someone DM's you on Instagram? Have you ever received an emergency DM? ME NEITHER.
3. Do not look at your phone while you're in bed. Not before you go to sleep or when you wake up. Put your phone in a location that requires you to leave the comfort of your covers to look at it. Then challenge yourself to brush your teeth *before* you check your phone. I promise if an actual emergency had occurred while you were sleeping, someone would have called you. Have you ever received an emergency text or email? ME NEITHER.
4. You really want to know what's going on in the world? Check the news in the evening right before your family does that adorable "everyone go around the table and say something you're grateful for" thing or right before something else that's going to bring you back up after the news brings you down.

If the news or social media makes you feel stressed and anxious and overwhelmed and bad about yourself, why are you starting your day with it? Do you like those feelings? No, of course you don't, but you might be addicted to them. Did you know you can be addicted to anxiety? Or addicted to outrage? Or addicted to knowing how many likes you got on Facebook?

Is 5-Star Future You addicted to what other people think about her? Is she addicted to negative feelings? Or does she have an impact on the lives of others because she's able to use her creativity and strength and awesomeness to actually get something done around here?

You want to make a positive difference? Clear the crap from your brain and take action.

STRATEGY #4: IF YOU KNOW YOU NEED TO CUT SOMEONE OUT, CUT THEM OUT

I said I wasn't going to make you cut anyone out, and I'm not. I'm not living your life; you are. You are the expert on being you, so you've got to listen to that voice in your head that says, "This person is hurting me."

It might take a while for you to get to a place where you feel strong enough and confident enough in who you are to step away from those relationships. I worked with a coaching client named Jolene for over a year before she decided to take that leap. Here's what she has to say about what it took for her to finally accept that some of her family didn't need to be part of her life:

I was raised in a peculiar environment with a laundry list of strange and strict expectations that I just didn't meet. Those expectations came from the ideology of my town and religion but also from my family. I didn't realize just how deeply ingrained some of those irrational expectations were until I started to examine why my family made me feel so horrible and stressed out in the present. I always assumed there was something wrong with me that caused these people not to see me or express any sort of affection or interest in me.

The idea that it wasn't me, that I was worthy of the sort of love and affection that comes with family, slowly dawned on me after adulthood and work took me away from my hometown, but especially when I started to make connections with outside friends — people who truly and deeply shared my values, interests and goals. But I truly came to realize what family meant when I became friends with Sara — who quickly became my sister-from-another-mister and welcomed me as a part of her family in a way I'd never known before.

Through my friendship with Sara and as honorary aunt for her kids, my heart was able to understand what my head had been bashing fruitlessly up against for decades — that true family doesn't judge or diminish a member if they don't live up to an impossible set of criteria. True family loves unconditionally, takes an interest in each other's lives, and seeks to be together in good times and bad.

This hit me especially hard during a Thanksgiving Zoom chat with my family of origin... who basically treated me as though I were invisible. I was at Sara's house, and as soon as I left the chat and she asked me how it went, I burst into tears. She and my honorary niece, Amy, hugged me tight and told me they loved me, that I was so brave for going through everything I'd gone through in my life, that they'd seen how hard I'd struggled, and that I would always have a place with them. In thirty seconds, they acknowledged me on a fundamental level in a way that I'd been waiting for my family of origin to do for decades.

It was a powerful moment, and one that helped me let go of my own expectations of behavior for my family of origin. I needed to accept who they were just as much as I needed to be accepted for who I am. The realization was that I already had a family who loved me the way I needed to be loved; they just weren't the family I had been born into. Recognizing that and letting go of past expectations allowed me to proactively and positively shed the relationships that weren't working for me and to give my full energy to the ones that are.

I've allowed myself to stop attending events of my family of origin and worrying about meeting their expectations. Even after I explained my decision to step back, those family members still don't understand. It doesn't matter though because I feel happier and more at peace now than I ever have, and I feel so supported and useful as a family member with my found family.

No matter which of these strategies you try, there's something important you need to remember:

Other people's reactions have nothing to do with you.

Even if they are reacting to something you said or how you're pulling back or being less available, their reaction is about them, not about you. Remember the friend who didn't want you to cut out alcohol because of how it made *her* feel about *herself*?

There will be people in your life who see you growing and don't like it.

That's their problem, not yours. You are not in charge of other people's emotions, and when you allow them to have their reactions and act the way they want, you're letting them be themselves just like you want them to do for you. Don't fall into the trap of trying to turn them into who you need or want them to be. They won't like you trying to manipulate them any more than you like them manipulating you.

Maybe they'll see your hard work and growth and be inspired to become a more authentic version of themselves. Maybe they won't. Either way, you can only control yourself; you can't control whether or not people freak out about who you're becoming.

DID YOU GET THAT? CHAPTER RECAP:

- When you make a no-turning-back decision to become a truer version of Future You, the Universe is going to get to work right away helping you become stronger. It might feel like a setback, but this will be your first big chance to stand firm as the new version of you.
- You've got to start identifying who is going to be on Team Future You. Who is going to be on board with you growing, and who is going to try to hold you back?
- It might be that some of the closest people in your life are not going to support your dreams or the changes you're trying to make. That's okay. When you spend less time with those people, you make room for new, true friends to come into your life.
- For those people who are more likely to steal your energy and squash your dreams but you're not ready to cut out of your life, there are some strategies you can employ to reduce the damage:

☆ Be intentional about when you spend time with them.
☆ Don't tell them your dreams.
☆ Reduce the amount of noise coming into your brain from the internet.
☆ If you know you need to cut someone out, do it.

LET ME ASK YOU THIS:

1. Who in your life is already on Team Future You? Who lifts you up when you're down? Who makes you feel more energized and hopeful after you spend time with them? Who is there with honest feedback when you need it?
2. How can you spend more time with these allies and cheerleaders?
3. Who are the enemies in your life? Who leaves you feeling tired and drained? Who wants to shred your origami-bird dreams?
4. How can you be more strategic in the ways you deal with these people?
5. If you could create your ideal friendships, what would they look like? Use the questions in the journal to guide you.

CHAPTER 6: WHO'S DIRECTING THIS MOVIE?

When my husband and I got married, a lot of people started asking when we were going to have a baby. Friends and family, of course, but even people I barely knew would randomly ask me if I was pregnant.

It was uncomfortable to say the least. I'm the kind of person who is not particularly fond of being told what to do, so oftentimes it also made me unreasonably enraged.

After a while, I got tired of just saying no and changing the topic, so I started thinking of fun replies to shut them down. Things like…

"No, but I appreciate your noticing my weight gain."

"No, but I'll call you next time I get my period."

"No, but we just got a new mattress. Maybe that will help."

I didn't actually say those things, but I daydreamed about it. I know a lot of those people loved us and meant well, but the decision to have a baby or not is a pretty big one, and these people were making a huge assumption.

At no point had we said to any of them that we even wanted a baby. When we moved into our house, I painted my office a gradient of aqua to lime green (it's my office under the sea!) and when I was showing it to a friend, she said, "Oh, is this going to be your baby room?" To which I replied: "No. Why would I give my office to some baby I don't even *know*?"

I didn't feel the desire to have a baby even though woman after woman told me, "Soon your clock will start ticking."

People started handing me their babies when I walked into a room so I could "practice." Never mind that I'd had three younger siblings and I'd been a nanny for a baby.

I was chafing under the weight of these blatant expectations, but I thought my discomfort had more to do with not wanting to be told what to do than actually not wanting a baby. I didn't want to ruin my life just to prove a point to those people that they weren't the boss of me.

Maybe we should have a baby, I thought.

We talked about it and set aside a portion of our budget for saving for a baby, but I never really felt motivated to save the money. I accepted hand-me-down baby stuff from family members and shoved it into our attic. I started worrying about how I would keep my freelancing clients if I had to take time off for having a baby.

This went on for years until finally my husband and I realized *we didn't want a baby*!

It's not that we just didn't want to conform. It wasn't that we couldn't afford one. It wasn't that our clocks just hadn't started ticking yet.

We didn't feel the desire to have a baby. At all.

It felt like we were the first couple to ever come to this realization. We knew it was the right choice for us, but it still felt "wrong" by society's standards.

We didn't know it at the time, but this part of our journey would be the perfect example of how our dreams and desires (or lack of desires) are there to guide us and to execute the Universe's perfect timing.

We met our nephew's best friend a couple of years after making this decision. When we found out he was in foster care and would need a permanent placement, we felt called to adopt him.

If we'd had a baby when we were planning to, it would've disqualified us from becoming foster parents. Our desire NOT to have a baby is what led us to adopting our son.

There's nothing wrong with you for feeling the weight of expectations from your family, friends, and society. Your job is to discern which parts of those expectations align with your desires and what **you** want out of your life.

For lots of women, their family's expectation to have a baby is perfectly in alignment with their vision of a meaningful life. The majority of my friends wanted to have babies, and some of them went to great lengths to overcome infertility issues. They knew, without a doubt, they wanted to have kids.

For others of us, having a baby isn't something we even want, but we must sort through the noise to discern what is our desire and what is ingrained expectation.

STEP 1: CLARIFY THE EXPECTATIONS YOU ARE FEELING

Listen to your language when it comes to what you're supposed to do. My coaching clients usually start sentences with:

"As a parent, I'm supposed to…"

"I feel like as I woman, I should…"

"People expect you to…"

"Everyone thinks…"

Look for language that has to do with what other people expect of you (not what you expect of yourself… we're going to get to that in a different chapter). These answers are going to be unique to you, but you're going to think they aren't. You're going to think these are rules that everyone knows, but the truth is, the rules are different depending on where you grew up, how old you are, what kind of school and/or church you went to, and many other factors.

Each of my coaching clients expresses these expectations in different ways, but they all believe that's just the way it is. So no worries on whether or not the rules are universal. We're just looking for the spoken or unspoken expectations you feel.

STEP 2. PAY ATTENTION TO THE RULES YOU'RE FOLLOWING AND START ASKING QUESTIONS

Do I have to do this?

What would happen if I didn't?

How would I feel?

Do I want this thing I'm supposed to want?

You always have a choice, and your choices have consequences.

You don't **have** to go to work, but you **choose** to because you like the consequences of having a job, making money, and paying your bills.

You don't have to exercise, so maybe you don't. And then you get the consequences of being out of shape and struggling to walk up a flight of stairs.

My sixth grade teacher told us we didn't **have** to come to school every day, we **chose** to. Of course, Past Mel thought he was crazy. *He doesn't know my parents. I literally have to come to school. They would kill me if I didn't.* (not true)

You might be thinking something along the lines of "Mel, I have to take care of my kids."

No, you don't. There are hundreds of thousands of kids in foster care in the US, and some of them are there because their parents didn't take care of them.

You don't have to take care of your kids; you choose to. Maybe that's an expectation you've picked up from society, and living up to it **is helping you** live your version of your best life.

I'm not saying all expectations are negative. I'm just saying they exist. No one is making you fall in line with these expectations; you're doing that to yourself. And in some ways, it's working out great for you. In other ways, not so much.

> Just because you know the expectations doesn't mean you have to meet them.

To be clear, I'm not talking about bucking the system when it comes to society's rules about not murdering people or stealing their stuff. This whole book is about living in alignment with the Universe and fulfilling your purpose, which means hurting others is a no-go.

So now your job is to move forward in visualizing your 5-star life, knowing that you might feel internal resistance caused by the weight of expectations.

Maybe you're a born rebel, and your instinct is to think, "No one is the boss of me." In that case you, like Past Mel, have to determine "Is this something I truly don't want… or is it just that I don't like conforming and I'm going to deprive myself of something I want just to be different?"

Or maybe you're a people pleaser and rule follower, in which case you've got to quiet the noise and ask, "What appeals to me not because someone is telling me I should, but just because I feel drawn to it?"

In either scenario, slowing down and spending some time with yourself is key. Quieting the noise literally means taking some time to think. Read this book, journal about the questions, go for a long walk or a drive by yourself and simply think your own thoughts. I promise the answers are inside you; it's just that you may be so used to having constant input that you've forgotten how to listen to your gut instinct.

When we talk about creating Future You, imagine we're talking about a different person. She can be anyone you want her to be! She can be the kind of person who conforms to expectations or not. She can be, do, and have whatever you want. We're writing the movie where she's the hero, and she's amazing.

As we design this majestic character and write her story, do your best not to let those shoulds and supposed-tos hold you back from that vision of Future You.

DID YOU GET THAT? CHAPTER RECAP:

- Expectations exist, and we all feel them. They aren't inherently good or bad; they just are.
- The things you think you "should" do are controlling the choices you make. In some cases, those expectations are leading you towards your version of your 5-star life. In other cases, they aren't.
- As you become aware of these external expectations, you can begin to reduce their interference in creating your vision for Future You. You are creating the character of Future You, and ain't nothing or no one holding her back!

LET ME ASK YOU THIS:

Finish these sentences:

- There's no way I could ever stop…
- Everyone expects me to…
- I absolutely have to continue…
- The people at work would be mortified if I…
- My family would think I was crazy if I…
- My friends would be so upset if I…

Now you know a few of the many expectations you're feeling. Cycle back through those sentences and finish them as many times as you can. I left extra space for you in the journal.

CHAPTER 7: FUTURE YOU, THE SUPERHERO

I LOVE WATCHING the TV show *Caribbean Life*. I want to visit the Caribbean and own a house at the beach, so watching the show is like watching Future Mel's life. The beach is my happy place. I love how warm it is, how much time I get to spend outside, the sound of the waves, the majestic thunderstorms, the general lack of snakes, and the way everyone seems more relaxed because they're on vacation. I just love it.

Some might call *Caribbean Life* my "guilty pleasure." Which is a terrible term. Thanks, society, for telling me I should feel bad for liking what I like.

Sometimes we feel guilty for wanting what we want. Like there's something wrong with us for wanting a house in the woods or a condo at the beach or to be on a stage or to leave our corporate jobs and become puppy trainers.

There's nothing wrong with you.

As long as your ambitions don't involve hurting others, it's all good.

> We like what we like because we like it.

You don't need to judge or figure out why you like something. Just recognize that you're drawn to that thing and move forward with the assumption that this desire is meant to guide you on your journey.

It would be nice if designing Future You were simple. If I could say, "What do you want?" And then you could provide a dissertation on everything you desire.

It doesn't work like that though, because we get this conversation going in our heads that says things like:

Who are you to think you can achieve THAT?

You want WHAT? That seems weird.

I hope no one finds out you wrote that; they'll never let you live it down.

Oh no! Doing that would involve completely changing everything, and that sounds hard and scary. Pass.

And if the conversation doesn't bubble to the surface of your mind, believe me, it's still happening in your subconscious.

So I'm not going to ask you what you want. Instead, I'm going to ask you to help me create a character. I've been going on and on about how you're the hero of the story and you're on a journey just like superheroes in the movies. So let's not design Future You. Let's make a new character:

SUPERHERO YOU

Superhero You is clever, talented, joyful, amazing, beautiful inside and out… and not you. It's not about you right now, it's about Superhero You.

Writers often fill out a character sheet to get to know their characters before they start writing the novel or script or comic. I included these questions and space to answer them in your FREE journal, which you can download at becomingfutureyou.com/book. If you're not able to access the journal right now, write down your answers on your own paper or say them aloud as you move forward.

ABILITIES

We've got to start with the fun part. What powers belong to Superhero You? I mean anything… flying, X-ray vision, being able to channel lightning, moving things with your mind, running superfast… I promise I'll help you turn this into something useful, but for now, go nuts.

APPEARANCE

How does Superhero You look?

Hair color, eye color, skin color, height, weight, physique. Create a kick-butt appearance for Superhero You.

HEALTH

Imagine that body combined with those powers… how does Superhero You feel physically each day? What about emotionally? Mentally? What does it feel like to run around like that all day?

What kind of energy does Superhero You have?

How do you think Superhero You keeps in shape?

MISSION

Being a superhero is hard work: What keeps Superhero You motivated? Why keep fighting the villains and saving the people?

What is Superhero You's mission? Sometimes superheroes have to save the planet, and then save it again, and then save it again. Other times, they're trying to protect their family or a specific group of people.

What about Superhero You? Who or what is Superhero You protecting? What motivates Superhero You to get out of bed in the morning?

VILLAINS

No superhero story is complete without a supervillain. Who does Superhero You stand up to? What battles does Superhero You run towards instead of away from? Is it a giant purple guy with a golden glove? Or an evil global conglomerate? What does the villain want that Superhero You is absolutely not going to let him have?

HOME BASE

Even superheroes gotta take a nap every now and then. Where does Superhero You sleep? Where is that structure located? Africa? Asia? Rural Pennsylvania? Brooklyn? What does it look like? What does it feel like? Is it dark and mysterious or light and sunny? A small hut or a mansion? Or maybe a space ship? What kind of comfort items does Superhero You keep nearby?

SIDEKICKS AND ALLIES

Every superhero needs a buddy. Who can Superhero You rely on? And does that person go into battle with Superhero You? Or does he or she provide ground support from a distance? What are that person's abilities? What does Superhero You like about them?

When they're not out kicking butt, what do Superhero You and Sidekick do for fun? Do they have other buddies they like to hang with?

ENDORSEMENT DEALS

Charities and organizations are always looking for superhero representatives… who does Superhero You represent? Why that cause instead of the many other opportunities Superhero You has?

TRUE LOVE

Ahhhh… There's no romance quite like a superhero romance. Does Superhero You have a special someone? Who is this person? What are they like? Do they go on missions with Superhero You or wait at home?

NOBODY RIDES FOR FREE

Does being a superhero pay? I've never been clear on that, but I know for sure nobody rides for free. That secret lair is going to cost something for upkeep, and superheroes gotta eat and take their sweethearts out to dinner.

How does Superhero You make money? How much money does Superhero You have? What does Superhero You do with that money?

RECHARGING

Is there such a thing as superhero self-care? What does Superhero You do to recharge?

Take a moment to answer these questions in your journal.

I don't know about you, but I'm excited thinking about Superhero You. Think of the possibilities! Being able to fly! Having a secret lair on a cliff! Eating carbs with no consequences—what a great superpower!

I mean, that's *my* vision; you've got to create your own.

What do you think about your design for Superhero You? Pretty awesome? Would you watch Superhero You's movie or read her book? Would you find it interesting, engaging, exciting? If not, keep coming up with answers to the questions until you've got the best possible superhero you can imagine.

Now reread your answers or mentally review them if you didn't write them down.

What stands out as the most awesome?

Superhero You's home base?

Superhero You's powers?

The way Superhero You looks or feels?

You created your version of an awesome superhero, so there's probably a lot that stands out as amazing and desirable.

Are you ready for my big reveal?

Surprise! I tricked you into visualizing Future You. Mwahahahahahahaha! I know. I'm so clever, and you never saw it coming.

But Mel! I said my superhero could fly, and obviously that's impossible.

Oh no, my friend. You didn't just use the word *impossible*, did you? Think for a second how many things were once impossible but are now part of our everyday lives:

- Cars
- Planes
- Trains
- Spaceships
- Air fryers
- Laptops
- Cell phones
- Electricity
- Heated floors
- Microwave popcorn
- Internet fast enough to stream Netflix (remember dial-up?)

If someone who lived just a hundred years ago were suddenly dropped into our current lives, they wouldn't be able to comprehend all the advances.

Reality can be what you make of it, and what was once impossible can become possible in your lifetime.

You got an impossible dream? Make it possible.

That said, it might be a while before we can move things with our minds and channel lightning, so let's get some more useful details from your visualization. Maybe your dream to fly has more to reveal than just "Future You wants to be able to fly."

Maybe the reason you said Superhero You can fly is because you want to be able to travel wherever you want whenever you want.

Maybe you wish you didn't have to sit in traffic ever again.

Maybe your mom lives all the way across the country and you wish you could just pop over for breakfast on Saturday mornings without having to drive a hundred hours or book a commercial flight.

Well, now we know your ideal version of Future You doesn't have a commute, has freedom to travel, and visits your mom more often. Behold! Clarity!

Let's take another example. Let's say your vision for Superhero You can move things with her mind. Why do you think that skill is amazing? If you had the power to move things with your mind…

You wouldn't have to constantly bend over to pick up the kids' toys.

Hot coffee could appear on your bedside table every morning.

You could brush the dog, vacuum, send an email, and cook dinner all at the same time.

Now we know your ideal version of Future You doesn't have to pick up toys (maybe she has kids who pick up their own toys?), has enough time to finish all her to-dos without an impossible level of multitasking, and relaxes with a cup of coffee in bed in the mornings.

Sounds nice, doesn't it?

What about Superhero You's sidekick? Did you envision one? What was that person like? If he or she goes into battle with Superhero You, then we know Future You has friends who are in The Thing with her. Whether "The Thing" is personal growth or parenting or career ambition, Future You has people in her life who are supportive of the way she's powering forward with becoming an authentic version of herself.

What about Superhero You's mission and endorsement deals? How might that be telling you something about who or what in the world you want to help? What about the villain? That villain is probably perpetrating something you think is an injustice. What does that tell you about Future You's values?

Now it's your turn.

Go back through your answers and ask yourself:

What might this mean for Future Me?

What would I do with this thing?

How would it help me live more authentically?

I added an extended version of these follow-up questions as an exercise in the journal.

We're creating clarity around who Future You is: what her life is like, what she wants, who she spends time with, and what drives her. Seeking this kind of clarity can shake you loose from floundering around in the "I don't knows" of it all and help you get to know more about what you want out of your life.

Of course, you don't know everything about Future You! And you never will because what you want changes as you get more information. **Remember, the journey is the point.** It's not about setting your goals once and then achieving every single one of them. Pursuing the goals and using your dreams as guideposts are what propel you forward and help you create your version of a meaningful life.

Seeking clarity is going to become a regular part of your life, and the more you do it, the more you'll know. And as you take steps forward, the more information you'll have to inform your vision.

One thing we know for certain: you don't get clarity by waiting for it to magically appear. You've got to seek it, and there's no better time than now. Look over what you designed for Superhero You and start puzzling out what it means for Future You.

DID YOU GET THAT? CHAPTER RECAP:

- We like what we like because we like it. It would be great if I could just ask you what you want out of your life, and then you could answer it and off we'd go, but it's not that simple.
- As soon as we start to think about what we want, our brain starts kicking up a bunch of questions about whether or not it's okay to want that, whether we deserve it, and "who do we think we are to have such a big dream?" or no dream or "what's wrong with us?"
- Instead, we've got to create a character who is not you and then work backwards to see what the details of that character say about what you want.

LET ME ASK YOU THIS:

1. What stood out as especially appealing when you were designing the character of Superhero You?
2. How might those details be indicators of what you wish were true in your real life?

Use the journal or go back through this chapter and answer all the questions.

CHAPTER 8: THE VILLAIN ATTACKS

I'VE ALWAYS LOVED MUSIC, and since you know I wanted to be Garth Brooks when I grew up, it probably goes without saying that I've always loved singing. For a period of my adult life, I sang with a band at my church. As with any ensemble I've been part of, there was a delicate dance of competition. This person got more solos. That person was more expressive.

Maybe it's the nature of the arts or the nature of my acting background in which some people got cast and some didn't, but I couldn't help but rank myself against the other singers. And I ranked myself as *the worst singer on the stage*.

I told myself I was fine with that because it was just a church group and they weren't going to kick me out. I was singing praise music, hanging out with my friends, and having fun.

But the more I told myself I was the worst singer on the stage, the more I found evidence that my conclusion was true.

Well, another solo going to someone else. Makes sense since I'm not a great singer.

I messed up that harmony again. No surprises there.

Oh look… I messed up the words. That's about right.

The more I told myself I was terrible at singing, the worse I felt about myself and the less worthy I felt to stand on the stage with those other people. It got to the point where I was holding back tears on Sunday morning when I was supposed to be singing my heart out and letting the Spirit move me.

So I did the only thing I could think to do. I quit.

> The greatest challenge you will face in becoming Future You is the voice inside your own head.

It's not the haters who bring us down. It's not the negative reviews of our service or store or products or books. It's not the mean things the other moms say.

It's that we hear those things and agree with them. As Eleanor Roosevelt said, "No one can make you feel inferior without your consent."

INTRODUCING THE VILLAIN

We're constantly telling ourselves stories about who we are, what we deserve, how we should be treated, and what we're capable of. And those stories, also known as beliefs, control the actions we take. And since actions control who you become, your beliefs control whether or not you become 5-Star Future You.

When you were analyzing your answers to the questions in the previous chapter, what sorts of emotions bubbled up?

Maybe you felt excited or nervous.

Maybe you wrote something down and immediately felt bad or wrong or dirty for wanting that thing.

Maybe you were gleefully imagining your future when all of a sudden, a voice in the back of your mind piped up and said, "Who do you think you are? You can't have all that."

That tiny voice is the villain who lives inside your head!

These stories will not only hold you back from becoming 5-Star Future You, they'll keep you from even visualizing your authentic life.

As long as we're telling ourselves a particular story, even if it's not helpful and depresses us, we're going to work consciously and subconsciously to make sure it's true.

Why? Because…

WE LIKE TO BE RIGHT

And because we like to be right, we're always looking for evidence that our stories are true.

Once I decided I was the worst singer on the stage, I looked for proof of my belief: I didn't get that solo, I made some mistake, I started singing at the wrong time. I didn't look for evidence that I was doing okay. I brushed off the compliments. I ignored the people who told me how much my presence meant to them. I never volunteered for a solo because that would go against what was becoming an ingrained belief:

I was a bad singer and didn't deserve a solo.

Our stories are running our lives. They might be things like:

I'm a terrible mother.

I'm a good problem solver.

I'm always late.

I'm funny.

I'm not enjoyable to be around.

I'm impatient.

I always find the best parking spots.

I'm just not good at math.

Some of these stories are helpful and empowering. Things like, "I'm smart" and "I'm fun" give you confidence. Other stories like "I lose everything" and "I'm short-tempered" keep you stuck and hold you back from becoming the authentic version of you and tapping into your limitless potential.

As long as you believe you're not good at something, you won't be good at it. As long as you believe you're destined for failure, you will be.

IT'S NOT YOUR FAULT

When Tiny Past You was picking up these stories, she was just trying to keep from getting kicked out of the herd. Safety was paramount, and fitting in was important because four-year-old Past You couldn't fend for herself. So she picked up these stories as guidelines on how to fit in.

She paid attention without discrimination to your parents, teachers, siblings, TV, church, and any other input. She watched for nonverbal cues and listened to what was said and came to childlike conclusions. For example, if Tiny Past You was singing the same song at the top of her lungs over and over and your tired, overwrought mother told her to stop, Tiny Past You didn't have the ability to think, "My mom's just tired today; I should give her some space." Nope.

Tiny Past You would've made some sort of conclusion like "Singing is annoying," or "My singing is bad."

And now that story is stored in your head.

It's not your fault that you have these stories; Tiny Past You was doing the best she could with the little experience she had.

You wouldn't yell at a four-year-old for not understanding the complexities of financial management, would you? Then don't get mad at Past You for listening to your parents fight about money and concluding that talking about money is stressful.

You might not even know that you believe talking about money is stressful. It could be that belief is buried so deep in your subconscious you don't even know it's there.

But even though you're not walking around thinking about how stressful it is to do financial planning, you're still looking for evidence that it is, in fact, stressful.

It's not your fault. You like to be right. I do too. We all fall prey to confirmation bias, so when it comes to the stories you're telling yourself, the ones you know about and the ones you don't, you're always on the lookout for proof that they're true.

YOU FIND WHAT YOU LOOK FOR

Past You might have picked up these stories, but Present You perpetuates them by continuing to look for evidence that they're true so you can be right.

We'd rather be right than be in a good relationship. Just think about how many fights boil down to not what's best for the couple but who is right. We'd rather be right than be comfortable or successful or happy.

Which means unless you do something different, Future You is going to have the same limiting beliefs trying to keep you safe from failure, disappointment and the possibility of getting kicked out of the herd. It's not your fault you picked up these limiting beliefs, but whether or not you perpetuate them… that is on you.

You find what you look for.

If you believe you're disorganized, you'll constantly lose things and miss appointments.

If you believe you can't run, that one time you try will be hard and you'll give up even though you consciously know it's going to be hard because you've never done it before. You'll just think it's harder for you than for anyone else and that's why you should quit. Or you'll remember you have bad knees and shouldn't run. Or you'll find four articles on the internet talking about how terrible running is for you.

If you believe you're not worthy of success, you might work hard toward your dream of being a published author, but every time you get close to finishing a manuscript, you'll scrap it and move on to a "better" idea, leaving you in a perpetual state of "aspiring" author. Or maybe you'll just never find time to write. Or maybe you'll talk about how you can only write when inspiration strikes, and you haven't heard from your muse in a while.

You find what you look for. If you're determined to become 5-Star Future You, you'll find a way. If you're not, you'll find a million and one justifications as to why you can't. There will be lots of things along the journey that you won't control, but you'll always have the power to control your thoughts. Here's your chance to harness that power.

FLIPPING THE SCRIPT

The great news about "you find what you look for" is you can flip the script. Once you start catching yourself perpetuating the unhelpful stories, you can change them. You're writing this movie, after all.

1. PAY ATTENTION TO YOUR THOUGHTS

You might be thinking, "Mel, I've got no idea why you're nattering on about limiting beliefs. I didn't think anything while I was visualizing Future Me."

Of course you had thoughts, my friend. You just weren't paying attention to them. You're thinking things all day long. You've had a lifetime of practice talking to yourself because you are always with you.

What's it like when you talk to yourself?

Are you kind?

Are you a jerk to yourself?

Are you a cheerleader?

Do you berate yourself for every mistake?

You might not be consciously aware yet of how you treat yourself, but in the days ahead, you're going to start paying attention to what you say to you.

2. PAY ATTENTION TO WHAT YOU SAY ALOUD

You're also going to pay attention to what you say to other people. Listen to the words coming out of your mouth and pay special attention to any sentences that start with "I am…"

Do you put yourself down in conversation? Is it a joke but also… not a joke?

"I'm late to everything. I'll be late to my own funeral."

"I'm such a klutz."

"I can't get my act together."

Look out for words like:

I can't…

I'm not…

I'm terrible at…

It's not just me who knows these are the no-no words. My friend Colleen goes to a gym where anytime they get caught saying "I can't," their coach makes them do ten burpees. If you don't know what a burpee is, just believe me that it's a particularly torturous whole-body exercise that involves putting your face too close to a smelly gym floor.

3. PAY ATTENTION TO HOW YOU RESPOND

You don't control everything that happens, but you always have the ability to choose your response. So how you are you responding to those stressful moments…

When someone cuts you off in traffic?

When you're running late?

When you stub your toe on the bedpost?

When your kid spills her juice for the fourth time in the past hour?

When you're just trying to finish this one email and your husband interrupts to ask what you want for dinner?

How do you respond? Do you fly into a rage? Do you take deep, calming breaths? Do you clench your jaw and grind out "I'll take care of that in a minute, honey"?

4. ASK YOURSELF, "IS THIS HELPING ME BECOME 5-STAR FUTURE ME?"

Start looking at all of it—your thoughts, your words, your responses—through the filter of whether or not it's helping you become Future You.

Would Future You lose her mind and scream at her four-year-old?

Would Future You throw herself on her bed in a fit of tears after stubbing her toe?

Would Future You let out a stream of curse words that would make a sailor blush after that individual cut her off in traffic?

Would Future You talk to herself that way? Would she call herself stupid?

Would Future You say she's not a runner when her dream is to run a marathon?

I don't know the answers, but you do. Are your thoughts, words, and responses helping you or hurting you in your quest to become 5-Star Future You? Your job is to start noticing the difference between what Future You would say and do and what Present You is currently doing.

5. WRITE A NEW STORY

Once you identify one or more of those beliefs that are not helping you become 5-Star Future You, you can rewrite them into stories that will empower you and then start looking for evidence that your new stories are true.

When I thought I was the worst singer on the stage and took what turned out to be a three-month hiatus, I worked on this very thing. What's the opposite of thinking you're a terrible singer? Thinking you're a good singer. But it's not like I could just start telling myself I had a lovely voice and expect to believe it. Instead, I asked the question:

What if I'm actually a **good** singer?

Can I find any evidence that might be true?

I dug in my memory and remembered that time a nice lady had come up to me and said how much she enjoyed seeing me on the stage. Then I thought of that woman who always sat in the second row and told me she just loved my voice and wished she could listen to me for hours. Then I reached way back in my memory to college when one of my professors complimented me on how far I'd come vocally.

You might be thinking, "Mel, if all this really happened, how could you have thought you were a terrible singer in the first place?"

Because I was looking for evidence I was a bad singer, not a good one! Remember, I was ignoring the compliments and brushing away the proof that contradicted what I believed. I had to dig around in my memory to find those examples. This process took three months, and even then I didn't really believe it yet. Believing it took another two years of telling myself I was a good singer and looking for any possible shred of evidence that supported my new claim.

Changing your beliefs isn't a quick process, but it's possible.

Let's walk through another example. Let's say your limiting belief is that you don't know what you want out of your life and you never have.

ME: Is that really true?

YOU: Yes.

ME: What about when you were a kid? Can you think of anything you wanted when you were a kid?

YOU: Yes, I wanted a pony.

ME: Why?

YOU: I thought it would be fun to ride really fast and have an animal who loved me.

ME: Can you get a pony now?

YOU: No, I don't think it'll fit in my apartment.

ME: What about finding a riding stable where you could take lessons?

YOU: Oh yeah, maybe I could do that.

ME: So is it true that you don't know a single thing you want and you never have?

YOU: I guess not.

ME: So maybe you could start digging around in your memory for other things you've wanted over the years and look for more evidence that your limiting belief isn't true?

YOU: I also really loved the ocean that one time we went on a school trip when I was in high school. I thought it would be cool to live there. I guess that's another thing I wanted.

ME: Yup, you're on a roll now. Keep going.

Now it's your turn. You're going to listen to your thoughts and to the words you say aloud. You're going to pay attention to your responses, and you're going to look for those beliefs that tell you that you can't have your ideal life. Then you're going to question them as if they're on trial.

You're going to ask yourself... can I find any evidence this isn't true? And because you find what you look for, when you look for evidence to debunk your limiting beliefs, you'll find it. It might take time and you might have to dig in your memory, but I promise the evidence is there. I've yet to challenge myself or a coaching client with this assignment and have either of us come up empty.

Once you find even the tiniest shred of evidence, write a new TRUE statement that you want to carry with you in your journey to becoming Future You. It might be:

I'm becoming a better singer with every rehearsal.

I am capable of running.

I can achieve anything I put my mind to.

I am a calm, patient mother.

You don't have to believe the statement yet; that's going to take time. But write it on a Post-it and attach it to your bathroom mirror or set a phone alarm that goes off three times a day with your new statement. After just a couple of weeks of doing this, one of my students declared me a genius because it was already working. (Thanks, Reba!)

This can get overwhelming fast, so if you're new to this, pick ONE new statement and work on it for a few weeks until you've at least got it memorized. Then add the next statement.

If you're thinking that these statements sound an awful lot like the hippy-dippy affirmations you've heard of... yes, boo, they're affirmations, but don't make it weird. An affirmation is just something positive or *affirming* that you say to yourself on purpose. We're working on being kinder to YOU here!

We're going to keep working with these in the chapters ahead. The most important thing though is that you actively look for evidence that supports your new, empowering beliefs. If you're going to become 5-Star Future You, you're going to need beliefs that remind you of all the ways you're a magnificent creature working to become the 5-star version of you.

DID YOU GET THAT? CHAPTER RECAP:

- The greatest villain you will face in becoming Future You is the voice inside your own head.
- You didn't create the voice, but you perpetuate her power by repeating unhelpful stories to yourself like "I'm not smart" or "I'm not good with money."
- You like to be right (just like the rest of us), so you're walking around looking for evidence that your stories are true. And because you find what you look for, you find the evidence you need, mark the story as true, and continue to perpetuate it.
- Once you identify one of your stories, you can flip the script and replace them with more empowering beliefs.
- To do this, you're going to need to start paying attention to what you say to yourself, what you say to others, and how you respond in stressful moments.
- When you find a story that you're repeating, you can analyze whether or not it's helping you become 5-Star Future You. If it isn't, you can write a powerful new story to replace it.

LET ME ASK YOU THIS:

1. When you make a mistake, what do you say to

yourself? Make a list of the things you're mostly likely to say inside your head or under your breath when you mess up.
2. When you're talking to others, what sort of things do you say *about* yourself? Make a list of every "I am" statement you can remember saying.
3. What's your go-to response in stressful situations?
4. Look at each of your previous answers and ask yourself the question "Is this helping me become 5-Star Future Me?" Sort your notes into two lists: "Helping Me" or "Holding Me Back."

TAKE ACTION:

- Pick one of the stories that's holding you back from becoming 5-Star Future You and rewrite it into a more helpful belief. (Reread Step 5 for examples.)
- Take that new story and write it on your bathroom mirror or tape it to your steering wheel or put it in your phone as an alarm. Keep repeating that story until you've got it memorized and looking for evidence that it's true becomes a habit. This might take a while, and that's okay!

CHAPTER 9: UNLOCKING & EMBRACING YOUR POWERS

When I was ten, I wrote a story called "Rumplemixup." It was about a girl going on a road trip to visit her grandparents and taking all her favorite books with her: *Cinderella*, *Rumpelstiltskin*, *Little Red Riding Hood*, *Snow White*, and *Rapunzel*. While the girl's family was traveling, the basket she used to carry the books tumbled to the floor and all the stories got mixed up. Meaning the dwarves had to kick Rumpelstiltskin out of their house and Little Red Riding Hood kept trying to sneak into Rapunzel's tower to take a nap and Snow White wouldn't let Cinderella have her glass slippers back.

And then my teacher published it.

I mean, she gave me and the rest of the class card stock on which to draw our covers, and then she stapled the whole thing together into a book. It was a magical experience, but more importantly, Mrs. Fallert told me that I was a good writer.

That summer, I wrote another children's book about going to pick out a Christmas tree. It didn't get published in card stock or otherwise, but a seed was planted that said, "I could be a writer."

Like a lot of heroes, I ignored my instincts, stopped writing, and didn't pursue publication again for almost thirty years. Instead, I put myself in supporting roles: library assistant, author assistant, marketing assistant. Always the assistant; never the author. I succumbed to the lie so many of us believe:

I've got nothing special to offer.

So many of us succumb to one of the first hurdles of being a hero—thinking we're not special, we don't have anything to offer, we don't have unique gifts… We're just kind of here, trying not to take up too much space.

YOU'VE GOT SPECIAL POWERS

The Universe loves you and wants you to prosper, and in order to help you on your journey to prosperity, however you define it, the Universe gave you special and unique talents. You've got a combination of gifts no one else on earth has at this exact moment.

Think about how many people you've met in your lifetime.

Have you ever met anyone who looks exactly like you down to the mole hidden in your left eyebrow?

Have you ever met anyone who has all the exact same thoughts as you and expresses them in the exact same way?

Have you ever met anyone who has the same number of siblings, grew up with all the exact same influences, and also became a doctor, just like you?

Of course you haven't, because even if you and your doppelganger started out similar, you still had different life experiences, met different people, learned different jokes, picked up different skills, and became completely different people. My husband is an identical twin, and even though he and his brother share DNA, they're completely different people with different personalities, skills, interests, and passions.

You can give two hundred authors the same starting idea for a book, and they'll all write something different.

You are the only you.

I'm writing what's probably the one millionth published personal-growth book in the English language, but I'm still writing it my way in words only I can use because I am the only me. And for some of you, my words and explanations are the exact ones you need to hear at this point in your life.

And knowing the Universe was guiding me in writing this book took a huge burden off me. *If you don't like one of my examples, take it up with the Universe!*

But really, if you can believe in something higher than yourself, everything is less burdensome. It doesn't matter what you call that force, just that you believe that this greater power loves you and wants you to live a joyful, meaningful life. This belief will instill in you a hope and optimism and peace you can't achieve any other way.

This greater power made you of love, and love isn't ugly or disgusting or garbage, so how could you be? The Universe made you uniquely awesome so that you can use your gifts and talents to fulfill your place in the world.

UNCOVERING YOUR POWERS

This can be a challenge, especially if you've spent most of your life telling yourself the story that there's nothing special about you and you've got nothing to offer. (Oh look, it's one of those limiting beliefs we talked about in the last chapter!)

Let's think about this...

If the Universe loves you, wants you to be happy, and gives you the desires of your heart, then we have to assume your desires are meant to be guideposts.

This was a hard one for Past Mel to learn. I thought the Universe wanted me to use my talents in ways that would make me miserable. I knew I was smart, so I assumed the Universe wanted me to be a doctor. I would be capable of it; I would also hate it because blood makes me angry. (And queasy... but mostly angry... what's it doing on the outside of someone's body when it belongs on the inside? *Get your act together, blood.*)

But I thought since I was capable of being a doctor, that had to be what the Universe wanted me to do.

I also spent a brief period thinking I was supposed to be a nun because I couldn't think of anything that would make me more miserable.

The Universe doesn't want you to be miserable! Unless your desires involve actively harming yourself, your relationship with the Universe, or other creatures, they're not wrong.

Your desires are there to guide you in the journey to becoming Future You.

PRESENT YOU

Present You's desires are there to help you discern your innate gifts, talents, and superpowers. You'll likely still have to work hard to develop them, but your interests tell you where to put your focus.

Love being around kids? Okay, great... That tells you something about your talents and points you in a direction of where to go next. Somewhere around kids.

Love talking to people one-on-one? Perfect... Now you know you need to get yourself into more situations where you can work with people one-on-one.

Love painting? Get thee to the craft store and buy some supplies! And possibly find someone to give you lessons.

What skills has Present You worked hard to develop in the past five years? And, more importantly, do you enjoy using those skills? Note I said "using" those skills, not cultivating them. Cultivating anything can be hard and a lot of work, even if it's something you enjoy. But when you actually get to use your skills, no matter what level they're at, and you see the impact it makes and feel the joy it brings into your life, that can be a magical level of rewarding.

What activities bring you joy? Is it spending time with people you love? Snuggling puppies? Walking in nature? Watching funny movies? Is it making homemade cards and mailing them to your friends?

What kind of compliments does Present You receive? Does anyone ever tell you you're so...

Organized?

Clever?

Funny?

Creative?

Good at coming up with solutions?

Great at talking to people?

Amazing at making quiche?

Start listening to those compliments, and when you receive them, instead of brushing them off, say "thank you" and think about how being good at that thing might be a guidepost to becoming Future You.

Now keep in mind, people say some crazy things, so if one of these "compliments" doesn't ring true, give yourself permission to brush it off. Especially if the compliment is followed up with some sort of "you should…" life advice. Sometimes that sort of unsolicited advice can give you great insight. Other times, it'll leave you scratching your head or worse, spinning out over what you should do versus what you actually want to do.

Why do you think Kiddo Past Mel thought of becoming a nun? Someone told her she should.

KIDDO PAST YOU

Kiddo Past You was less weighed down by shoulds and supposed-tos and limiting beliefs about what was possible. So revisiting the desires of your childhood can start to shake loose some of your authentic interests.

We know Kiddo Past Mel enjoyed writing stories. We also know she wanted to be Garth Brooks when she grew up. One of these is really easy to translate into something useful: Kiddo Past Mel liked to write—Present Mel should maybe consider writing.

The other example is going to take a bit more interpretation. Obviously, I can't grow up to be Garth Brooks because there's already a Garth Brooks. So now we have to ask, "What did Kiddo Past Mel like about the idea of being Garth Brooks?"

He had a wireless microphone.

He entertained large crowds.

People cheered for him.

He got to be on a stage with really cool lighting and, occasionally, pyrotechnics.

So what does this tell us about Mel's innate interests? She likes entertaining people, loves applause, and thinks "on stage" is an awesome place to be. Present Mel probably has some natural talents when it comes to talking to groups of people, cracking jokes, and commanding attention.

Just because I'm not going to be Garth Brooks doesn't mean that dream is useless. It still provides guidance and causes me to ask, "Do some of my natural superpowers align with this desire?" Those are superpowers I should give some attention to and ask how they might play into my current and future life.

What about you?

Think back to Kiddo Past You. What was she interested in? What did she want to be when she grew up? What did she think was fun? What sort of "play pretend" games did she like? Who did she admire?

What are your childhood dreams trying to tell you about your current (maybe undeveloped) superpowers?

SUPERHERO YOU

If you look back at Superhero You… what kind of villains did she fight? Who did she help? What problem did she solve for the world?

Even this exercise that might seem silly has something to reveal for you. Your answers are going to be different than anyone else's because they're going to be informed by your innate desires and interests.

If Superhero You fights the Puppy Bandit, a villain who uses his X-ray power to magically age all the puppies in the world into adult dogs so no one can ever feel the joy of puppy snuggles, that tells you something. Maybe it's that you think it's important that everyone have the opportunity to experience the unrestrained excitement of a puppy just learning to play tug of war. Maybe you think everyone deserves the chance to laugh and feel the joy a pet can bring. Maybe you want to help bring that joy to others. Maybe you want to make sure people in nursing homes, who had to leave their pets behind, get the opportunity to still snuggle with a dog.

Even Superhero You is trying to get you to embrace your talents and use them to help others.

THE UNIVERSE NEEDS YOU TO STEP UP

You are special and unique and powerful. You are the only you, and your desires are meant to guide you into your using your talents to fulfill your role in the world.

Have you ever been grateful that some people feel called to be kindergarten teachers because that is definitely not for you?

Or thanked the heavens some people want to be doctors because you'd rather amputate your own toe than amputate someone else's?

We all gotta do different things! My path is different than yours, which is different than your sister's. If I hadn't finally gotten around to embracing my talent for writing, you wouldn't be reading this book.

What is the world missing because you haven't embraced your powers? Because you're busy hiding in someone else's role? Because you believe you're supposed to be miserable?

Or if "the world" seems too big, what are the people in your inner circle missing because you're refusing to embrace what makes you uniquely you? That weird, quirky sense of humor? Your ability to throw incredible parties? Your special skill for making anyone feel loved and appreciated?

What are we missing because you think "anyone can do" what you do?

Anyone *can't* do it! But *you* can! And you love it!

You no longer have the excuse of saying no one ever told you that you were special and have something to offer. I'm saying it. It's time to unlock your gifts, embrace your powers, and move forward in your journey of becoming Future You.

DID YOU GET THAT? CHAPTER RECAP:

- The Universe loves you and wants good things for you.
- Your desires are yours for a reason, and unless they involve harming yourself or others, they're not wrong.
- You've got special gifts and talents that no one else will use and express quite the way you will. You are the only you!
- Your interests, desires, and dreams are there to guide you in recognizing your unique gifts and talents. If you like doing something, that's a big clue!
- The Universe needs you to step up and use your special skills to help others. No one else can take your place.

LET ME ASK YOU THIS:

1. What are you interested in learning more about?
2. What activities bring you joy or make you feel alive?
3. What skills has Past You worked to develop that you enjoy using?
4. What kind of compliments do you receive from others? What do people tell you you're good at?
5. What did you like to do as a kid? What were you interested in? What did you dream of doing as an adult? Who did you admire?
6. Even if that dream seems wrong for you now, what elements hold clues as to your natural gifts and superpowers?
7. How might Future You enjoy using those talents?

CHAPTER 10: THE MISSION

I was one of those annoying kids who always wanted to know *why*. My poor parents and teachers and grandparents and other random adults... I know I was that annoying kid who was always asking questions, but it wasn't a stalling tactic or because I didn't know how to have a conversation. I just really liked to know the thought process or reasoning behind things.

My mom and I would have conversations that went sort of like this:

MOM: We're going to the grocery store.

TINY MEL: Why?

MOM: Because we need groceries.

TINY MEL: I accept this logic.

Obviously, the need for food was acceptable. Plus I liked hiding in the circle clothes racks when we went to Walmart, so I was pretty much down with grocery day. Things were less great when we had conversations like this:

MOM: Clean up your room.

TINY MEL: Why?

MOM: Because I said so.

MEL: Hmmmmm…

In the absence of sound logic, I'd create my own. *She told me to clean up my room, but she didn't have a good reason, so I'm just going to shove everything under my bed, call it good enough, and get back to reading Nancy Drew.*

You know how parents wish their children will have kids with the same annoying habits they used to drive their parents crazy? My mom got her wish. When my son came into our lives, he was also one of those kids who had to know why, why, why! It was so frustrating!

THE BATTLES

It's not just me and my son… knowing why can be exceptionally motivating. Whether it's:

Why you're bothering to exercise… *because you want to be flexible enough to get on the floor and play with your grandbaby.*

Why you're cleaning the house… *because your friends are coming to visit.*

Why you're walking the dog… *because you want her to live a long, healthy life.*

Why you're trying to start a podcast… *because you want to reach people with your message.*

Why you're getting up early to write your book before starting work… *because you want to achieve your dream of being published.*

We know that every choice you make has consequences, even if they're tiny. Every action or inaction is shaping you into a version of Future You. You're almost never in a situation where you "don't have a choice," it's just that sometimes the best choice is so obvious you forget there are other options. You don't have to go to work, but you prefer the consequences of keeping your job and continuing to get paid. You don't have to clean your house, but you prefer the consequences of your friends feeling comfortable in your home instead of sitting on the couch and being coated with cat hair.

Big whys and little whys are another way of saying "so I can…"

I exercise so I can play with my grandbaby.

I walk the dog so I can keep her in my life for a long time.

I publish my podcast episodes so I can help women uncover their potential.

Knowing why we're doing the hard work helps us keep our goal and the consequences of our actions in mind. When we know why, we can tap into a source of motivation that's unique for us.

> Your whys are personal and that's what makes them so powerful.

I don't have any grandkids, so your why of playing with your grandbaby isn't going to get me to exercise. But for you… you love that little booger, and you want to be in her life as long as possible. She and any other grandkids you might have in the future are motivators. You'd like to attend her high school graduation, walk down the aisle at her wedding, and hold her first child, your great-grandbaby, in your arms. So that's why you're doing the weight training even though it's hard and uncomfortable and it makes you feel silly to be lifting those five-pound weights when the musclehead next to you is bench-pressing a tractor tire.

You're doing it for sweet little Delia, the world's most adorable child.

Wow! That's a strong WHY! I don't even know Delia, and I'm tempted to hit the gym with you.

Think about a goal you're working towards. Maybe it's something you've thought of since you started reading this book; something that will help you bridge the gap between Present You and your vision of 5-Star Future You.

Why does it matter to you?

How will achieving that thing improve your life?

What might you learn along the way?

What will Future You have that Present You doesn't?

Becoming Future You is no easy task. Each goal, each action, each habit, takes you closer to becoming 5-Star Future You, and they all take work. Each step is a battle in the overall mission of creating your version of a meaningful life. When you have a clear vision of what you're working towards and why it matters, that vision will keep you going when things get difficult.

Let's say you've realized that Kiddo Past You really wanted to be an author, but Adult You shelved that dream because it's not realistic to think anyone can make a living as an author. (Oh look! It's another limiting belief. I personally know seventy-two people who make their living writing books.)

So now that you've realized Kiddo Past You wanted to be a published author and you can see how that dream fits into your vision of Future You, you're ready to take that goal off the shelf and get back to work on it. Let's clarify your WHY:

MEL: Why does the goal matter to you?

YOU: It was always a dream of mine to be published. I just gave up on it, I guess.

MEL: How will achieving that thing improve your life?

YOU: Well, for one thing I'll know that I didn't give up on myself and my dreams. Plus people will read my book, and that will be cool. And I might even make some money, which I could put towards paying down my car.

MEL: What might you learn along the way?

YOU: How to write a book and how to publish a book.

MEL: What will Future You have that Present You doesn't?

YOU: A finished book!

MEL: Finish this sentence: I'm going to write and publish a book so that…

YOU: So that I can feel proud of myself and prove to myself that I can do it… So that other people can read my words… So that I can make a little extra money and so that I CAN BE A PUBLISHED AUTHOR!

For someone else, having strangers read their words might be a nightmare, but for you it would be a dream come true. Hang on to that why, and when you're frustrated or it seems too hard or you just want to quit, remind yourself why you're doing it… so that you can get your story into the world and achieve your dream of being a published author.

If you feel your motivation flagging when it comes to a goal or a new habit, ask yourself…

Why am I doing this? How am I helping Future Me?

THE MISSION

Superhero You had a mission. What was it? Was it protecting all the puppies of the world? The women? The kids? Your kids? Freedom of speech? Was it destroying all the weapons your company created that have been sold under the table and are now being used by the bad guys to hurt innocent people?

Superhero You's mission tells you something about your instincts: who you think deserves help, what you view as an injustice, what you want to protect.

This give us some insight into one of your Big Whys.

The Big Why is often called a mission statement or purpose statement. You might think it's only companies that need a mission statement, but you need one too. Or rather, you already have one. You just might not know how to put it into words yet.

There's something driving you, pushing you forward, getting you to read this book. Do you know what it might be? When I work with my coaching clients, sometimes they've got an answer right away and other times it takes me asking, "Why? Why? Why?" until we reach something that feels right.

Here are some of their answers:

I'm becoming the best version of myself to honor and serve my Creator.

I'm on a mission to teach women to unlock their potential, fulfill their purpose, and live a meaningful life.

I want to be a good mother so that my kids will be successful, happy, have strong relationships, and ultimately thrive.

When I write, I feel like I'm fulfilling my purpose.

I believe many people feel unsafe, and I write books to make others feel, safe, loved, and capable.

I work hard to provide for my family.

My Big WHYs are to be an energetic, joy-filled, FUN person who empowers everyone around her and helps them be the best versions of themselves. And to care for myself in the manner I deserve so I can be giving and empathetic toward others without them draining me dry so I have nothing left to give.

I want to help heal broken people in ways that provide them hope and meaning. I want to use the talents God gave me to make a difference in the world and for people to find solace in me.

Meaning and purpose are things we crave as humans. We want to know what we're doing matters—that WE matter. You might not have the words to express what that means for you, but the instinct is still somewhere inside your heart.

When you work on clarifying your MISSION or MISSIONS (yes, you can have more than one, and yes, they might change as your life changes), you're able to use that clarity to filter decisions and guide you in becoming Future You. For instance, let's say your mission is to make everyone you encounter feel loved, appreciated, and worthy of respect, and I ask you to take a bag of dog poop and set it on fire on my neighbor's porch. You'll be able to run that decision through your mission statement and come to a conclusion that aligns with your values.

You'll be able to say:

I really like Mel, and I want to be friends with her, but I also want everyone to feel loved and respected. It seems like a flaming bag of dog poo would make Mel's neighbor feel disrespected. That's the opposite of what I want. Nope! Sorry, Mel. I'm not going to do that for you.

Excellent choice! You passed my very clever test.

I know that example seems ridiculous and unlikely, but think about how many decisions you make every single day: what to eat for lunch, how to respond to your kids, what to say or not say during the watercooler gossip session. Knowing your MISSION makes all of that easier to navigate, which makes it take up less energy, which leaves you with more energy for doing the work to become 5-Star Future You!

DEFINING YOUR MISSION

There's no one true way to create a mission statement for yourself. I've seen giant questionnaires online, listened to podcasts that asked only a few questions, and read a book where the author said he just sat on the beach for a day and journaled about it until he came up with an answer.

Here's my take on it, but know that however you come up with a sentence or two that feels good to you… that's correct. And since you can have more than one, and they might change over the course of your life, it probably goes without saying that you can revise this at any time. The only thing you can't do is revise a blank mission statement, so challenge yourself to come up with something.

Answer these prompts in the free companion journal or on your own paper. You can download the journal at becomingfutureyou.com/book.

Let's look to 5-Star Future You for some guidance. What do you want people to say about her at her funeral?

"She always made me feel…"

"You could always count on her to…"

"I never doubted that she cared about…"

"She taught me to…"

"She inspired us to…"

"She really made a difference by…"

And let's bring Present You into the picture as well:

What bad things or injustices have you heard about that absolutely infuriate you and make you wish things were different?

What do you wish more people knew?

What do you wish everyone could feel?

What would you say are your top priorities?

What are your values?

And now we bring it all together:

Whatever stood out to you most in your previous answers—whether it was the way Future You made people feel or something you identified as your top priority or that injustice that infuriates you—*what would 5-Star Future You do about it?*

Would she write books where the characters overcame that hardship? Would she volunteer at a charity that assists people with that struggle? Would she give a TED Talk about it? Would she teach her kids how to treat people better? Would she use her influence at church to start a fundraiser?

What would the 5-Star version of you do about realizing her top priority is her family? Would she make sure her family knew how much she cared and that she would do anything for them? Would she demonstrate that with her words and her actions? Would she adjust her schedule so she was able to spend more quality time with the people she loves?

What about if you just realized the thing you most want is for people to be inspired by the way you live your life bravely and go after your dreams without apology? Would you start filtering every decision through the question of "what kind of example am I setting?"

I know this isn't an exact template, but that's because mission statements are as unique as we are. No two are exactly the same or carry the same weight and meaning. This is something you're going to have to work for; it's not going to come down from the heavens perfectly defined on a stone tablet.

You might try a freewrite using any of those questions as prompts. One of my coaching clients told me that freewriting is always her least favorite assignment and the one where she learns the most. A freewrite is simply:

1. Setting a timer for the amount of time you want to write (at least five minutes).
2. Picking a prompt like one of the questions above or a question in your own mind.
3. Putting pen to paper and writing until the timer goes off. You don't worry about grammar or punctuation or making sense. You just keep writing without pausing. Let me say that again because it's important:

don't pause to think! Just keep writing. If you don't know what to write, write the words: "I don't know what to write," and by the time you finish that sentence, the next one will have formed in your mind.

Once you complete your freewrite, read what you've written. Some of it will seem like absolute gibberish, but other parts will make you say... "What!? I didn't know I thought that."

When you freewrite like this, you're able to jiggle loose ideas from your subconscious that your conscious mind normally blocks.

Once you do your freewriting and answer my questions and take a day to sit on the beach to think about it (optional), distill your mission or missions down to a few sentences that mean something to you and clarify *what* you do and *why* you do it.

The WHY is your mission and the WHATs are your current strategies. It might be that Future You discovers those strategies aren't working as you planned, so she may pivot to other things, but the mission could remain the same.

WHAT: I work hard to provide for my family. (strategy)

WHY: So they can feel safe and loved and lead fulfilling lives of their own. (mission)

WHAT: I create books, courses, and podcast episodes. (strategies)

WHY: So that women will understand that they have unique and special gifts and so I can encourage them to use their talents to help others. (mission)

WHAT: I write books and lead groups and mentor people. (strategies)

WHY: So I can help heal broken people in ways that provide them hope and meaning, so they can find solace in me, and so I can use the talents God gave me to make a difference in the world. (mission)

It's all about you, so there are no wrong answers here, and you can revise your mission at any time. If you're thinking about saving this for later, please don't. Your mission is not going to just come to you in a flash of inspiration. Or at least mine didn't, and I waited for years and years and years. Answer my questions, do the freewrite, reflect for a day or so, and then WRITE SOMETHING DOWN. Actually write it down on paper and put it in a place you can see. I'm not saying you have to get it tattooed on your body just yet, but if you can't write it on your hand in washable ink, you're not done with this step.

MAKE IT MEAN MORE

Once you have a draft of a mission statement, you've got to lock it in. Say it to yourself every morning when you wake up and every evening before you go to bed, write it on your bathroom mirror, put it on a Post-it on your car steering wheel, make it your background photo on your phone, write it on every page of your planner, put it across the top of your kanban board. Find ways to remind yourself over and over and over of your mission statement. Just because you write it once doesn't mean you're going to remember it. You've got to practice remembering it.

And then you've got to add emotional weight to the words.

I had a professor in college who always gave the same feedback to every actor after every scene:

"Make it mean more."

Every actor. After every scene. And we were only doing Shakespearean plays in that class, which were very much not my jam. One day I was sick, but I'd dragged my butt to class because I was a kid who didn't miss, and it was my day to perform.

After my partner and I finished our scene and sat down, Kevin opened his mouth to give us our notes, but I raised my hand and said:

"Let me guess. Make it mean more?"

My fellow actors thought it was hilarious, but even today I'm cringing over how obnoxious that was. Sorry, Kevin. I didn't mean it. I was high on cold medicine that day. And Kevin *was right*!

Even though his feedback wasn't that creative, he did teach me an important lesson. Not only do we need to know what we want, we have to make it mean more.

You've got to take the words of your mission statement and not only repeat them, but you've also got to imbue the words with emotion. You've got to say the words aloud and feel them in your gut and in your heart. You've got to really think about what you're saying and start building this vision of Future You who lives with integrity and meaning and authenticity guided by the words of your mission statement.

And as a side benefit, the more you say the words, the more you'll realize, "Oh, this word isn't quite right, I'm going to change it." Or "This sentence needs a little tweaking."

You're never going to be done seeking clarity on Future You, whether it's your MISSION or what you want or what limiting beliefs are holding you back. Becoming Future You is a lifelong process. You're answering the questions in this book now, and if you come back in six months and do it again, you'll come up with clearer answers.

The students in Unlock Your 5-Star Future, my DIY coaching program, get lifetime access to the course material, and some of them went through it once, waited a year, and then went through it again. They told me things like "I didn't realize how many 'shoulds' I was still including when I wrote my answers the first time."

That's because *it takes time and purposeful effort to get to know your authentic self*. It doesn't happen overnight, and it surely doesn't happen by waiting for inspiration to strike. As you move forward, you'll start shedding that peer pressure and you'll start asking why you think things have to be this way or that. You'll grow and change, and so will your answers. That's all part of the process! You can't "set it and forget it" when it comes to growth. It's only in going forward that you can see more of what a meaningful life is going to look like by your unique definition.

You're on your way. You've gotten some amount of clarity, and now we're going to take that clarity and run with it.

DID YOU GET THAT? CHAPTER RECAP:

- Knowing why you're working can be incredibly motivating, whether it's regarding a small habit like putting away the clean dishes every morning or a big goal like cleaning out your garage. When you know your personal WHY for pursuing that goal, you'll feel more motivated to do the work associated with it.
- Even if you don't know how to define it, you're on a bigger mission. There are reasons you get out of bed

in the morning; there are forces driving you and your actions.
- When you work on defining your mission or missions, you're able to use what you know about yourself to make choices that align with what you believe.
- Defining your mission takes purposeful effort. Answer my prompts, do the freewrite, take a few days to think about it, and then write something down. Seriously anything! A mission statement that feels sort of okay but you're probably going to revise it later is better than nothing at all.
- Once you have your mission statement, you've got to memorize it and imbue it with emotional weight. Make it mean more!
- Just like the students in my course, you'll have to keep digging and coming back to the questions in this book and answering them with new perspective to get closer and closer to your authentic self.
- If you want to get clarity faster, join Unlock Your 5-Star Future. I'll give you the training and worksheets you need to give this whole becoming Future You thing a giant jumpstart. Find out more at becomingfutureyou.com/unlock

LET ME ASK YOU THIS:

1. What do you want people to remember about you when you're gone?
2. What sort of impact or influence do you want to have in the lives of others?
3. What frustrates you or do you wish were different in your small circle or the world at large?
4. What would you say are your top priorities?

5. How do you act on your top priorities? What actions do you take?

Don't forget, I included these and additional prompts in your free journal.

TAKE ACTION:

1. Write your first draft of your mission statement. Don't worry; you'll revise it later.
2. Put your new mission statement on a Post-it and place it somewhere you'll see it every day.

ACT III: BECOMING FUTURE YOU

CHAPTER 11: STEPPING INTO THE ROLE

When I was a kid, I fell down a lot. I don't mean metaphorically; I mean I tripped over things constantly, took dramatic tumbles in the yard, bumped into anything or anyone near me, and fell while walking *up* the stairs from the basement nine times out of ten. My dad had built our house and always insisted he made that one step taller than the rest. He was joking… I think.

Either way, my family started calling me "Grace" and I started thinking of myself as a klutz when what I really wanted to be was a dancer.

This was in my "I want to be on stage so bad I can taste it" phase as I'd moved on from wanting to be Garth Brooks specifically to wanting to be like Debbie Reynolds and Barbara Streisand, starring in movie musicals. The movie musical hadn't made a comeback yet, but ten-year-old Mel was convinced it was coming. (She was right.)

I begged for dance lessons despite clear evidence that I was less than graceful. My parents finally relented after I got my license and could drive myself.

Fortunately the studio didn't place teen me in beginner ballet with a bunch of four-year-olds and I never had to wear pink tights.

There was evidence all around me that I was klutzy and about ten years too late in getting started to really make any headway before I'd need to move to LA and start auditioning, but I got up early every morning before high school and rehearsed my tap numbers on our porch even when it was thirty-two degrees outside and my toes were freezing. Oh, and the rest of my family was trying to sleep. Sorry, guys.

I didn't realize it at the time, but I was stepping into the role of Future Mel. In my mind, Future Mel was an amazing dancer and amazing dancers have to rehearse all the time. So that's what I was doing. I was acting like the person I wanted to be.

ACTING RULE #1: KNOW WHAT YOUR CHARACTER WANTS

As an actor, one of the first steps in taking on a new character is learning what the character wants. Not just their overall objective, but how the thing they want is driving everything they say, everything they do, and every tiny movement they make. You can't walk ten feet to the right unless you know why the character is crossing the stage (to pick up this cigarette or to get to a better view of the secret locket being worn by the other character in the room).

Do you know what we've been doing throughout this whole book?

Figuring out what Future You wants.

Now that we know some (but definitely not all) of what Future You wants, you can start to act like her. You can work on stepping into the role of 5-Star Future You. You can ask yourself the question:

WHAT WOULD FUTURE ME DO?

Walk around your life with this question running through your mind for an entire day.

The alarm goes off. What would Future You do? Get up and put on her workout clothes, hit Snooze, or grab her phone and scroll?

Some of your friends are chatting at the watercooler at work. Would Future You join in, change the subject, or keep walking?

It's time to make dinner. Would Future You make a salad or order pizza? Or maybe both?

Dinner is over and the kids are in bed. Would Future You grab her laptop and work on her novel for thirty minutes, engage in one of her hobbies, or grab the remote and turn on Netflix?

I don't know the answers here, but you do. And if you don't… what an excellent opportunity to create more clarity around this character of Future You.

Hmmmm… Would Future Me eat pizza or a salad on a Wednesday night? I guess to figure this out I'm going to have to think about what kind of health Future Me has. Maybe Wednesday is her pizza splurge night. Or maybe she eats healthy during the week and only cheats on the weekend. Or maybe she makes healthier homemade pizza. How will this hypothetical pizza affect the running routine I know she has because somehow she manages to run a 5k even though I've never run unless something was chasing me?

Start noticing what's different between what Present You naturally does and what Future You, the most authentic version of you, would do.

The characteristics of Future You are never going to come in a flash. It's in asking question after question and weighing your options that you start to get clarity on who Future You is and what she would do.

It's in asking the questions that you embrace your new identity. It's in clarifying what Future You would do and say and think that you can start to say…

I AM FUTURE ME

Your actions are what turn you into Future You, and do you know what's largely controlling your actions? Your beliefs.

Despite evidence to the contrary, I believed I was a dancer, and so I acted like one. As a result, I became a much better dancer.

What you believe to be true about you is running the show when it comes to what you say and what you do. Do you remember those limiting stories we talked about earlier? The ones *the villain* inside your head has been telling you?

I am not a runner.

I am stupid.

I am a klutz.

I am always late.

I am scatterbrained.

I am terrible at accepting compliments.

Since you read that chapter, I know you've been listening for those stories—the ones you say out loud and the ones that you only say to yourself. The ***limiting*** beliefs are the ones that don't align with Future You because they're the ones holding you back from being your authentic self.

You've been rewriting those stories *into something that Future You would believe*, or stories that give you strength and power and allow you to be more and more of your authentic self.

They might be things like:

I am strong.

I am smart.

I am loving.

I am a problem solver.

When you adopt one of Future You's stories or "I am" statements, you take one more step into the role of Future You, and for the rest of your journey, you'll weigh the question "I know I am a smart, loving, problem solver. So what would a smart, loving, problem solver do in this situation?"

As you move forward, your job is to work on adopting Future You's specific beliefs and actions.

What would Future You say?

How would Future You talk to herself?

How would Future You handle this situation?

What would Future You do?

Would Future You believe that you're strong and smart and capable and talented and have unlimited potential?

In repeating our stories to ourselves, we continue to make them true. (*Look how right we are!*) When I told myself I was klutzy, I tripped on everything. When I told myself I was good at memorizing routines and I was the kind of person who got up early to rehearse, I became a better and better dancer.

BATTLES

It's human nature to choose short-term gratification over playing the long game. Of course we'd rather eat cheesecake today than lose ten pounds in a year. Ick. A year is SOOOO LONG. *Just give me my cheesecake already!*

> You're going to face constant battles between what Present You wants to do and what Future You *would* do.

But your life is a long game. And at the end of it, what are you going to say you're glad that you did or experienced or achieved?

Those are the actions Present You needs to start taking today. Which means you've got to start adopting Future You's beliefs today instead of waiting and hoping you just wake up one day and discover you magically transformed into the most authentic version of yourself overnight through no effort of your own.

Some of your goals and dreams are going to take years of work. Others will take less time than you think—definitely less time than you've been putting off doing them. Past Mel had a dream to publish a book for about twenty-seven years. Once I finally got my head on straight enough to write it, the whole process took about nine months.

The process of becoming 5-Star Future You is a lifelong journey, but you won't have to wait until the end of your life to start seeing the benefits. Maybe Present You is chronically dehydrated, but you decide Future You drinks half her body weight in ounces of water every day. It might only take a week of drinking that much water before you feel the difference in your energy level and see it in your skin.

The time is now.

The hero is you.

Now that you know who Future You is, act like her.

DID YOU GET THAT? CHAPTER RECAP:

- Throughout this book, we've been gathering information on what you want and who Future You is. Now that we know more about her, you can work on becoming her.
- Start carrying these questions in your mind:

  ☆ *What would Future Me do?*
  ☆ *What would Future Me say?*
  ☆ *How would Future Me talk to herself right now?*
  ☆ *How would Future Me handle this situation?*

- As you get to know more and more about Future You, you can adopt more and more of her beliefs. When you know Future You is a calm, patient mother, you can use that knowledge to influence Present You's decisions and actions.
- Becoming 5-Star Future You is going to take effort, but some of those dreams and goals and characteristics are going to be achieved quicker than you expect once you put your mind to it.
- And no matter how long the dreams take to achieve, you'll start seeing the benefits of living intentionally right away.

LET ME ASK YOU THIS:

1. How would 5-Star Future You talk to herself when she makes a mistake? What about when she achieves a victory? How is that different from the way you talk to yourself now?
2. How would Future You handle that difficult person at work?
3. How would Future You handle that frustrating thing that keeps happening at home?
4. What's one healthy habit 5-Star Future You has that Present You doesn't? Hang on to your answer as we move into the next chapter.

TAKE ACTION:

1. Set a phone alarm that goes off once a day during the part of the day when you know you're usually not at your best. Label the alarm WHAT WOULD FUTURE ME DO?
2. Open your planner, and at the beginning of each week write the words, WHAT WOULD FUTURE ME WANT ME TO WORK ON THIS WEEK? If you use a digital calendar, set a repeating Monday appointment with the same question.
3. If you haven't done so already after reading the chapter about rewriting your stories, pick one "I am…" statement that you know Future You believes and write it on a Post-it or twenty and put it somewhere you'll see every single day.

CHAPTER 12: HABITS

I'VE ALWAYS HAD excellent dental-hygiene habits. I remember to floss more often than not, and I never go to bed without brushing my teeth. As my college friend Jackie says, "Night is when the bacteria has a party in your mouth."

Ew.

This is why I was so shocked recently when my dentist told me my gum line was receding.

What! Impossible! I have such good habits!

Honestly, I was outraged. Between my brushing routine and my lucky draw in the genetics department, I'd only ever had one cavity, and the filling is so small I don't even know which tooth it's in.

"Right," he said. "You do have great habits, which is why I can tell which side of your mouth you start brushing on. You're making more strokes on that side and pressing harder. That's where your gums are receding."

Booooooo, Past Mel! Her meticulous brushing habits have turned me into She of the Sensitive Teeth.

Depending on which study you read, 40–90 percent of what you do is a habit. How much you eat for dinner, the order you wash your different body parts in the shower, how you respond to other drivers in traffic, how easily you get overwhelmed, whether or not you're always angry... Habit.

Even on the low end, that's a lot of your daily life.

Which can lead us to only one conclusion: the habits that you have now are creating Future You. That includes the positive and the not-so-wonderful: Will you be Overbrushed Teeth Future You? Gets Winded Walking Up the Stairs Future You? Or maybe Finally Sold Her Pottery at a Craft Fair Future You?

Past You's habits created the life you're living today. If you've had an exercise habit for the past few years, you're stronger and healthier as a result. If Past You had a habit of always losing her temper with her kids, Present You's relationship with them might feel a bit strained. If Past You developed:

A meditation habit, then you're calmer.

A writing habit, then you have a finished book.

A buying lunch every day habit, then you've got less money.

A staying up too late every night habit, then you're always tired.

A hitting Snooze eight times every morning habit, then you're always late.

A seeking clarity on Future You habit, then you know more about who you want to become and are likely living with intention and purpose.

It's not just the obvious things that are habits. It's how you feel about yourself, how you talk to yourself, how you respond and react to stressors, and whether or not you treat your day like an opportunity or something to slog through.

Those limiting or liberating stories you tell yourself… Habit. Looking for the evidence that you're a terrible mother… Habit. Looking for proof that you are good at your job… Habit. Looking in the mirror and being grateful for your good skin… Habit.

Your habits are controlling who you're becoming, plain and simple. This is great news for us because it means we have a simple strategy to use in the journey of becoming Future You.

OPTION 1: ADOPT FUTURE YOU'S HABITS

In the last chapter, I asked you to think of something Future You is doing regularly that Present You currently isn't. Maybe you know Future You says kind things to herself, but Present You talks to you as if you're the dumbest person she's ever met. That's a simple thing to change. Simple, but not easy.

If you want to be that version of Future You, you're going to have to develop a habit of saying nice things to yourself. Sure, at first you'll still habitually call yourself stupid for dropping a whole jar of honey on the floor again, but you can always follow it up with something positive:

"It's okay, Self. You're doing the best you can."

"You can always buy more honey. This not a big deal."

"I'm proud of you for only saying three curse words instead of your usual eight."

Maybe your vision of Future You is calm and patient with others even when she's tired and hungry when she gets home from work. That means you're going to have to develop a habit of remaining calm when you get home from work. Sure, at first you might still fly off the handle when you walk in the house and immediately step in cat vomit, but you can always follow that up with a few deep breaths and work on channeling Future You's inner calm.

Do you already know something about Future You's habits? Pick one thing to work on, and in a minute I'll teach you how to install that habit.

OPTION 2: ASK YOURSELF, "WHAT HABIT CREATES THAT ACCOMPLISHMENT?"

Maybe Future You has achieved or experienced something that you haven't yet. Maybe Future You owns that beach house you've always wanted or has a published novel or has an excellent relationship with her partner. Those are all wonderful things, but how did she get them?

To answer that, you'll have to make some guesses as to the process she might have taken to achieve those things. If she's got a beach house and you currently can't afford one, she must have more money. How did she get that? Did she win the lottery? In that case, she probably had a lottery ticket buying habit. Did she create a side business that earned enough extra income to cover the mortgage? Then she probably had a work in the evenings and/or on the weekends habit. Did she pare down her expenses so she could find the extra money? Then maybe she had a budgeting habit or a cooking at home instead of eating out habit.

If your vision of Future You includes someone who is strong and limber and able to walk the length of any parking lot without getting winded, how did she get that way? She probably has an exercise habit, and not just a going for a walk every day habit but some weight training to maintain her muscle mass. Maybe she has a yoga habit or a one-minute plank a day habit.

Maybe you're already in the health you desire. How did you get that way? And what habits do you need to maintain to stay that way?

Good health is one of those accomplishments that's always going to come from habits. You'll never just be able to achieve it and then walk away and expect it to be there when you need it. Same with friendships, relationships, mental and spiritual health, financial abundance… Okay, most things are not going to be achieve-it-once-and-then-you-always-have-it kinds of things. Most things require maintenance from healthy habits.

GIVE YOURSELF SOME CREDIT

This is the point at which some of my coaching clients get overwhelmed and declare, "I have a long, long, long way to go. I'm basically a disaster. I'll never become Future Me."

Slow your roll, babe.

> Present You and Future You already have some habits in common.

What are they? It's time to give yourself some credit for all the hard work you've done. You wouldn't have read this far if you didn't care about making some improvements and didn't believe they might be possible for you. So we know you have a learning habit and some optimism tucked in there as well. Good job!

What else? What other things do Present You and Future You have in common?

Are you a loving daughter and so is Future You? Hooray!

Are you super good at finding things? And Future You's kids are always so appreciative that Mom is able to find their lost shoe? Well done!

I'm serious about this. If you're feeling some feelings about how long this is going to take, please make a list of all the things Present You and Future You already have in common. Even before you were thinking about Future You, you made progress towards becoming her.

INSTALLING YOUR NEW HABIT

You could write a whole book about creating habits. As a matter of fact, many fabulous books have already been written on this topic, and I've linked to my favorites in the downloadable journal.

Instead of trying to teach you all the different ways you can install a new habit, I'm going to teach you the thing that irritates the students in Unlock Your 5-Star Future, my DIY coaching program, the most.

Pick One Thing

When you're getting started, pick only one new habit to install.

Some of my students get so excited once they've created their vision for their future, they want to install thirty-seven habits this month. Others feel like they're so far behind in becoming who they want to be, they want to install forty-two habits before next Tuesday.

Trying to make too many changes at once is a sure way to sabotage Future You. There's no way you can achieve all of those things at one time! And even if you get thirty-five out of thirty-seven new habits in every day, you'll still feel bad that you didn't manage to fit in the last two.

Eventually you can install all thirty-seven habits, but for now just pick one.

When in doubt, pick a habit that's related to your health, like exercise.

Then you'll want to…

Set Yourself Up to Win

If you have never had a daily writing habit but you've decided that's the one you're going to develop, don't plan to write fifteen hundred words every day. I know we've been talking about developing Future You's habits, but you've still got to start where you are. If Future You runs three miles a day and you run zero miles a day, you can't start with three. You've got to work your way up to it. Pick something small enough that you can actually accomplish it starting where you are. If the goal is to run three miles a day, maybe you start with walking for ten minutes a day. If the goal is to write fifteen hundred words a day, maybe you start with fifty words a day.

If Past You struggled with installing new habits because you insisted on trying something too big straight out of the gate and you don't believe me that you need to start small, read *Mini Habits* by Stephen Guise. That book will convince you that it's okay to start where you are and you're more likely to succeed if you do.

Make it Convenient

Whatever your new habit is going to be, make it convenient. If you want to exercise in the mornings before work, pick out your workout clothes the night before and put them in the bathroom. If the new habit is eating vegetables for a snack, precut your veggies and put them in snack-size baggies. That way they're as easy to grab as the bag of chips.

You can also attach your new habit to a habit you already have; this is called habit stacking. If you want to add five minutes of meditation to your day, do it immediately after you turn on the coffeepot, something you do without fail every single day.

Give Yourself Credit

Whichever habit you decide to install, find a way to track it. Maybe this means you buy a wall calendar and put a big X on each day you do the habit. Maybe you put a marble in a jar every time you do the habit, or better yet… a dollar. Maybe you give yourself a sticker in your planner every day. Whatever method of tracking you use, make sure you actually see it every day. This is why I'm fond of the wall calendar. Sometimes you might forget to do the habit, but then you walk by the calendar and remember, "Oh right! I haven't done my twenty jumping jacks yet today." And then you do them and mark your X.

Seeing that you're doing The Thing is so important with new habits because you might not otherwise see or feel progress right away. It takes several weeks of jogging before you start to feel your muscles tighten and notice that you don't feel quite as much like dying in the first minute as you did when you started, but you can always look at your calendar and see "Hey look! I AM doing The Thing! Yay, me!"

. . .

Develop Patience

How long will it take to install your new habit? Honestly, the science is all over the place. Some say twenty-one days. Some say it depends on the complexity of the habit. Some say it depends on the person. I say do it until you stop thinking about it.

For example, I hate skipping my exercise routine. It's not just that it's a habit, I feel weird if I don't do it. Even if I don't like the exercise itself, I like the way my body feels after I've done it. If I don't work out or stretch, I spend all that day missing the feeling. It would be like skipping brushing my teeth and thinking all day that my teeth feel furry.

You'll know your new habit is solid when you do it on autopilot or when it feels weird not to do it or when you crave the feeling the habit will give you.

You'll know it's a habit when you do it habitually. (obviously)

Then you get to pick a new habit to install and start the process all over again. Yay!

Being Future You

Becoming Future You is about installing the habits and beliefs of Future You. Being Future You comes about when those habits and beliefs become your truth. (Of course, by then you'll have another vision for Future You because that's how this works. You have unlimited potential, which means there's always going to be room for growth.)

Those "I am" statements we talked about in previous chapters—eventually saying those to yourself will become a habit. That's why I told you to write them down and put them on Post-its and set a phone alarm. That's why you're using them as... *gasp!*... affirmations.

And now you're going to develop habits that go along with those statements. You're going to say, "I am healthy," and then you're going to take your vitamins. And that vitamin-taking habit is going to be proof that you ARE healthy. So when you say, "I am healthy," you'll start to believe it more and more because you're looking for proof and—dangit—you're taking your vitamins! And hey, you do have a little more energy. And also you've been sleeping a little bit better. Hey, you are healthy!

> It's all a related cycle: what you say, what you do, and what you believe.

We're leveraging the power of that cycle turn you into Future You.

Some people say doing the habit is what changes your mindset and makes that new thing part of your identity. You start exercising regularly, and then you're able to say, "I am fit." Others say changing your identity is what causes you to change your habits. You say, "I am healthy," and so you stop eating a quart of ice cream for dinner every night because you are healthy and a healthy person wouldn't do that.

Which comes first? I know I've done it both ways. I changed my identity after a friend tricked me into starting a running program with her. I kept huffing and puffing my way through those intervals with her until one day I noticed it was getting easier, and I thought, "Hey... maybe I am a runner."

I've also changed my actions after working on changing my identity. At one point, I was the most miserable, negative person I knew, but I started every day saying, "I am a positive person. I look for the best in every situation." I didn't believe it for a long time, but then I started to notice I *was* looking for the opportunities in most situations. I *was* starting to sound more optimistic. I *was* feeling a bit happier. *Maybe I was becoming a more positive person!*

> Either way it happens, your actions and your identity are permanently linked.

You're rewriting your stories, and you're not only looking for proof that they're true, you're creating that proof with your habits. You find what you look for and what you create.

One way or another, for better or for worse, you're becoming Future You, molding who you will be with your thoughts and actions. Now you can purposefully *choose* both; step by step, you'll become more and more of your authentic, powerful, unlimited, superhero self.

DID YOU GET THAT? CHAPTER RECAP:

- The majority of what you do each day is habit.
- This means if you want to become 5-Star Future You, you're going to have to develop her habits.
- Before you get overwhelmed about how far you need to go, give yourself some credit—Present You and Future You already have plenty in common!
- What you do, what you say, and what you believe are all connected. We know you find what you look for, so we're setting you up for success by developing

habits that will be proof of Future You's positive identity.

LET ME ASK YOU THIS:

1. What habits do you think Present You and Future You have in common? Make a list.
2. What habits do you know Future You has that you don't currently do? Make a list.
3. Even though you certainly don't know everything about her, what are some things you think Future You has accomplished? Make a list, and then for each item, write down what habits might have created that accomplishment.

TAKE ACTION:

1. Pick one new habit that you want to install. Eventually you're going to need to adopt more than one new healthy habit, but we're only picking one for now.
2. Once you've selected a single habit to install, make it small enough to reasonably accomplish daily, make it convenient by attaching it to one of your current habits, and decide how you're going to track your progress.
3. Start your new habit today and mark your first X on your calendar (or however you decided to track).
4. Whatever you do, don't get in the habit of sabotaging yourself. Go on to the next chapter and I'll help you with that.

CHAPTER 13: STOP SABOTAGING FUTURE YOU

When I was in college, I wrote every paper the night before it was due. Didn't matter if it was supposed to be a five-page paper or a twenty-five-page paper, I started at about five p.m. and wrote until it was done. Or until the time to walk to that class came, at which point I printed whatever I had, turned it in, and then collapsed.

My high school teachers had warned me that method wouldn't work in college, but they were wrong.

I always got an A.

Every. Single. Time.

It was a terrible way to live, but I thought it was my process. Even though I tried to work on the papers in advance, I could never seem to make much headway until the deadline was basically choking me. As soon as the paper was assigned at the beginning of the semester, I'd start stressing. And I'd stress the entire four months until the night before it was due, when I'd write it while cursing Past Mel for screwing me over yet again.

Every hero has to fight battles, and you're no different. You're going to meet enemies along the journey, and you're going to have to fight them. Some will be people who want to hold you back and keep you small, but you're ready for that. Some will be those limiting beliefs that we talked about, but you're working on discovering those, rewriting them, and looking for proof of your new, powerful beliefs. In some battles, it might *seem* as if you're fighting an enemy, but it will just be the Universe helping you learn a skill or making you stronger.

Some battles though will be the ones you could've prevented, the same battle Past Mel fought over and over…

SABOTAGE… from Yourself!

Boooooo!

Can you think of any times Past You set you up to fail? Have there been times when you were in an uncomfortable, unpleasant, difficult situation, and on top of dealing with it, you were also thinking how easily it could've been prevented if only Past You had just gotten her act together!?

Sometimes you sabotage Future You because you just completely forget she exists. You're living in the moment, focused on the now, and totally ignoring any possible positive or negative consequences of your actions. This is especially likely to happen when you're tired or overwhelmed or hungry. Ever overeaten because you felt like your stomach was collapsing in on itself? But then thirty minutes later, you wished Past You had chewed a little slower and stopped sooner so you didn't have a food baby currently living in your stomach?

Sabotage.

Other times, you sabotage Future You because think Future You will be able to handle whatever it is you're putting on her plate. You think Future You has more time and is less stressed and will *definitely* be able to do that volunteer gig at your kid's school because that's so far away. September You doesn't have time for it, but you're certain November You will be able to handle it.

But then November You arrives, and she is just as busy, possibly more stressed, and now angry that Past You put this on her plate.

Sabotage.

The truth is, Near-Future You is a lot like Present You. She still has people who need things from her, she's approximately as busy as you are now and have been for the past few years, she's feeling a similar level of stress and overwhelm, and she's had other things come up that you don't even know about yet.

The first step to combating sabotage is to realize you're doing it.

So let's talk briefly about some of the most common forms of sabotage, and then we'll talk about a simple solution you can use for all of them.

PROCRASTINATION

Past Mel was a Master Procrastinator. I feel like I could've offered a certification program to teach people how to procrastinate quickly, efficiently, and with no regard for the future.

You might not be in as bad of shape as I was, but have you ever put off an important task for the weekend? Maybe the thing could have been accomplished if you'd worked on it for a couple of hours each night during the week, but you were just too tired. Now it's going to take all day Saturday and part of Sunday. When the weekend arrives, your friends ask if you want spend the day driving on the Parkway with them to see the fall colors.

You've always wanted to do that, but now you can't.

Thanks a lot, Past You.

> Procrastinating is deciding NOW what Future You is going to have to do with her time.

Procrastination takes away Future You's freedom.

We've been learning a lot about Future You throughout this book, but you're never going to be able to predict the future with 100 percent accuracy. Future You is going to have things come up that you don't see coming. Some of those will be great opportunities, but if you've filled Future You's plate to the max with all your procrastinating, she won't be able to take advantage of those opportunities, will she?

PERFECTIONISM

If perfection is what you're after, you'll never achieve your dreams.

It's that simple.

Is perfect possible? No.

But Mel. I just have really high standards.

I know you do, babe, but are your really high standards paralyzing you and keeping you from achieving your dreams? Have you been writing your first novel for four years and all you've got is a vague outline and a highly polished first chapter? Because you've got to get it perfect before you can move on to the next one?

Are you your harshest critic? Does the villain inside your head tell you your work isn't good enough and, by the way, you'll never be good enough either? And while she's at it, does the villain point out the flaws in everyone else too? Have you ever read someone's book, found it lacking, and thought, *"Wow. I mean, good for her, but I'm a perfectionist. I could never publish something like that."* Or seen someone at the store and thought, *"I could never go out in public without my makeup on."* Or visited Mel's house, seen the smoothie drips staining the cabinets from that time I forgot to put the lid on the blender, and thought, *"I know Mel's busy and everything, but I could never live that way"*?

Do you procrastinate starting projects because you don't want to work on it unless you have time to make it perfect? One of my Unlock Your 5-Star Future students once told me she won't clean her kitchen unless she has time to mop the floor, clean the counters, wipe down the cabinets, wash the windows and get out the toothbrush and clean all the grout on the backsplash.

So it's either perfect or it's nothing.

Either you clean all of the kitchen or none of it.

Perfectionism is sabotage in disguise. She lets us believe the lie that we're doing something good. We're not succumbing to sabotage; we just have high standards. We're just the type of people who have to make everything we do really, really, really, really, really, REALLY good. We can't live like those other people who just do things "good enough."

Perfectionism keeps us from using our powers by reminding us that we can't finish something unless it's perfect. We can't publish the book, launch the podcast, start the Etsy store, write the letter, apply for the job, finish the degree, take the family photos, wear the bathing suit, sing the solo, or finish the screenplay until it's perfect... until *we* are perfect. And even if we do achieve one of our goals, we can't enjoy it because it's not quite perfect.

And perfect isn't achievable, so I guess we're stuck.

Perfectionism keeps you from becoming Future You.

Becoming Future You is going to mean trying hard things, failing, learning, getting back up, cheering yourself on, forgiving yourself, and putting your imperfect self out into the world again and again and again.

You can either engage in the long-term sabotage of perfectionism that will keep you from even trying to achieve your dreams, or you can become the most authentic, but still imperfect, version of yourself.

IGNORING YOUR HEALTH

When we don't exercise, we don't get the benefits that come immediately following a workout—the better mood, the improved brain function, the stress release, the feeling of having stretched our muscles and loosened up some of those knots that showed up overnight. That's sabotage for Today You, but what about Tomorrow You and Five Years From Now You?

When we don't exercise over the long term, our muscles atrophy, our heart weakens, and we pack on extra weight. And the next thing you know, we've got a health condition that requires an expensive drug to mitigate.

Same thing with our nutrition. How do you feel on the days you eat cookies for breakfast? Shaky? Weak? Hungry again in forty-five minutes?

And what happens if you eat a bunch of garbage day after day for years?

Inflammation builds up. Hello, diabetes, heart disease, cancer.

I could play this game all day long:

Get enough sleep, have plenty of energy. Stay chronically sleep deprived, enjoy the anxiety and irritability.

Take regular breaks, experience improved focus and mood. Insist on constantly working yourself into the ground, enjoy being sick all the time.

Drink your water, feel better. Stay chronically dehydrated, have trouble pooping.

You don't need me to tell you to take care of yourself, but maybe you do need me to point out that you're not only harming Present You, you're also harming long-term Future You.

You can't put everything on pause while you're raising your kids, or give your whole life to your job and wait until retirement to focus on your health. By the time you reach that finish line, the damage to your health will be irreversible and you'll be wishing Past You had made different choices.

BLAMING PAST YOU… IS JUST MORE SABOTAGE

At this point, you might be thinking about all the ways Past You has sabotaged you before. Don't fall into the trap of beating up Past You for making mistakes. She was doing the best she could. She hadn't read this book yet, and even if she'd had an inkling she was sabotaging you, she didn't know how to deal with it.

That's not going to be a problem anymore.

THE SOLUTION: START DOING FAVORS FOR FUTURE YOU

Start paying attention to the ways you might be sabotaging Future You, or more likely, the ways Past You has sabotaged Present You. Feelings of regret or anger or thinking, "I wish I had…" are like flashing neon signs pointing directly to the moment of sabotage.

> You can't change the past, but you can influence the future.

Once you start noticing your sabotage patterns, you can work to disrupt them. If you're always procrastinating, start doing tiny favors for Future You around things you would normally procrastinate. Not just the big projects but the little ones.

I used to always procrastinate admin-related phone calls: things like calling the doctor's office, credit card company, vet clinic. I'd let it hang on my list and roll over day after day; even though it wasn't a big thing, it was still taking up some of my time to rewrite it over and over, and it was stealing my energy because I was dreading it and beating myself up for not doing it already.

And this was all over a phone call.

So if you're a Master Procrastinator, practice doing small favors for Future You on the little things. Just make the phone call or clean the litter box or send the email. Sure, you'll probably still procrastinate the big projects for now, but you'll start building up evidence that says "Maybe I'm not a procrastinator," and you'll work on resisting that limiting story that tells you that procrastination is part of your DNA.

> Start doing favors for Future You that combat your particular brand of sabotage. They don't have to be enormous changes to make a big difference.

If you keep eating cookies for breakfast, do Future You a favor and buy some protein bars next time you're at the store.

If you stay up too late night after night, set a "go to bed on time" alarm. And when it goes off, go to bed.

If you get winded when you walk up the stairs, walk up them every single day until you can do it without getting winded.

If you always miss your appointments, set as many calendar reminders and phone alarms as you need so Future You can arrive on time.

If you keep trying to perfect your podcast logo because you've got to get it just right, do a favor for Future You and just publish an episode already.

Future You isn't just going to appear and clean up your mess. She's not your maid.

You've got to do the work of becoming her and becoming the kind of person who does favors instead of sabotaging yourself. If Future You has plenty of free time, Present You is going to have to stop filling up her plate with all your procrastination and overcommitting. If Future You has projects finished and goals achieved, Present You is going to have to stop insisting that everything be perfect. If Future You feels calm, focused, energized, joyful, creative, motivated, or happy… *Present You has got to learn to stop sabotaging those things.*

And you learn by doing one favor after the next after the next after the next.

You won't be perfect, but you will be a *more authentic* version of you.

DID YOU GET THAT? CHAPTER RECAP:

- You'll face many challenges in your journey to becoming Future You. Some of them will be from other people, some will be the voice inside your head, some will be the Universe making you stronger, and some will be sabotage from yourself.
- Sometimes you sabotage Future You because you forget she exists. Other times you sabotage her because you think she'll be less busy, more organized, and generally better at dealing with life than Present You.
- The truth is, Near-Future You is similar to Present You and has challenges and opportunities come up that you don't know about yet. She's just as busy as Present You. Oh, and she's mad that you put something extra on her plate.
- The key to overcoming sabotage is to identify the specific ways you're setting up Future You to fail and then doing favors for Future You instead.
- Remember:

  ☆ Procrastinating is deciding now what Future You is going to have to do with her time.
  ☆ Perfectionism keeps you stuck and from becoming the most authentic, albeit still imperfect, version of you.

☆ Ignoring your health is short-term and long-term sabotage.

☆ Blaming Past You is an exercise in futility.

- If you're procrastinating, practice doing little favors for Future You to disrupt that procrastination. If you're stuck in perfectionism, practice doing some things good enough and then moving on. If you're ignoring your health, install a healthy habit.
- Get in the habit of doing favors for Future You.

LET ME ASK YOU THIS:

1. Off the top of your head, what are all the ways you know you've been sabotaging Future You?
2. What favors for Future You could you be doing on purpose to combat your particular brand of sabotage?

TAKE ACTION:

Do one favor for Future You within the next twenty-four hours. And this part is important—make sure you note that you're doing this thing as a favor for Future You. If you want to make something a habit, you've got to recognize that you're doing it.

CHAPTER 14: ENJOYING THE JOURNEY

"It sounds like you're going to have an exciting life."

It was a weird conversation to have with the receptionist at my eye doctor, but twenty-two-year-old Mel was always good at talking to people. I'd just graduated with my theatre degree, and I was going to Germany for the summer and then moving halfway across the country to South Carolina. I'd just told this receptionist in my tiny Midwest town as much, and she seemed amazed by my choices, as if I were doing something courageous.

Looking back on it, I guess it kind of was. At the time though, I felt a little lost. I had an aunt who lived in Germany and another one who lived in South Carolina. Both needed a nanny, and I needed a job.

After all, I was pretty sure I'd just wasted four years getting a completely useless degree.

But that receptionist was there to remind me: **it's not about achieving a specific goal or having your life turn out exactly as you expected; it's about enjoying the journey.** I wasn't moving to LA or New York to pursue acting like Past Mel had planned and I didn't know what I wanted for my future, but I knew my journey was taking me halfway around the world, and surely that would be cool.

Any hero's journey is going to include a lot of highs and lows and plot twists; that's what makes it interesting. You know your dreams and desires are guideposts to lead you forward in the journey. You know you're going to achieve some of your dreams, and that's going to be amazing. You also know you're going to pursue others and get a little way down the path only to realize that's not what you want at all. So you'll change course and move in a different direction.

It's okay to change your mind. It's not "quitting." You've been gathering information, and now you're redefining what you truly want.

Regardless, it's not the achievements that will make your life meaningful; it's the experiences. And not just having the experiences but enjoying them.

> If you don't enjoy the journey, you won't enjoy the achievement.

You've got to find joy in the work. You've got to find a way to embrace the challenges and use them to spur you forward instead of holding you back. You've got to remind yourself of the stakes; this is your life we're talking about.

Let me give you some strategies you can use to enjoy the journey.

1. GET SUPPORT

Heroes may seem to work alone, and some even take pride in proclaiming it, but if you pay close attention, they always have an extensive support system of sidekicks, allies, and mentors.

Sidekicks are those on the journey with you. Superheroes rarely charge into the-fate-of-the-universe-is-at-stake battles alone; they bring along any number of sidekicks and peers because even super soldiers need someone to watch their backs.

Your sidekicks and peers are those people who are not only interested in your growth but also in their own.

This Becoming Future You thing is a challenge and involves reflection and analysis and action; all of that is easier with someone by your side. It's like when you hear your mother's words come out of your mouth, and then you call up your sister to talk about it. Not only has she heard your mom say it, but she's heard *you* say it, and she's said it herself. She gets it.

You need people who are going to get what you're doing here. There are a few really easy ways to find these people:

1. Recommend this book to a friend and make sure you tell her you want to talk to her about it. And then actually talk to her. First of all, she'll have gotten different things out of it than you did. Second, if you've both decided to work on yourselves, you will have a common language to use. You'll be all, "I did a favor for Future Me today!" and she'll be all, "Nice job! Me too!"
2. Got a book club? Read this book with them and

contact me; I'll be happy to have a chat with your group!
3. Join our Becoming Future You Facebook Group. It's free, and we love encouraging each other. The link to join is in your journal. If you haven't downloaded it already, you can grab it at becomingfutureyou.com/book

Your allies are those people who bring you up, cheer you on, and encourage you.

They don't have to understand exactly what you're doing or even why you're doing it, but they love you and they want you to have a great life.

My grandpa lived most of his life on a Missouri farm that's now been in our family for over one hundred years. He never learned to use the internet, and he certainly didn't have any idea how I was managing to make a living on it, but he always asked me how business was going. He'd encourage me when I was feeling down and celebrate with me when I'd accomplished something big.

My grandpa said three things to me every time we said goodbye. He said, "I love you. I'm proud of you. I'm praying for you."

Exactly the words I needed to hear.

Who is this for you? Who loves you no matter what? Who wants what's best for you and is willing to listen to what you think that is instead of telling you what to do? If no one is coming to mind, start a running list of people who care about you and seem genuinely interested in how you're doing. These might be people you see in real life or people on the internet. They might be people who are currently in your outer circle of acquaintances, and it might be time to bring them into your inner circle of allies.

Your mentors are those people who speak the truth when you need to hear it.

They're the ones who will tell you to stop being so hard on yourself when you're going down the rabbit hole of blaming Past You. They're the ones who will tell you to be patient when you're wondering why this is taking so long. They're the ones who are willing to tell you to *get up* when you're more interested in *giving up*.

Who can you trust to be honest with you?

The roles are flexible; sometimes I'm the one who listens to my friend talk about how overwhelmed she is, and then I give her the tough advice to cut something from her life. Other times I'm the one crying on the phone, and she tells me the situation is hard, but it's time to get up and do something about it. My point is, don't feel like you have to run around putting the people in your life in the category of sidekick or mentor or ally. The only question you have to ask is:

Is this person helping me become Future Me?

Do they lift you up? Encourage you? Believe in you? Do you feel better after spending time with them?

If no one is immediately coming to mind for any of these categories, I know how you feel.

When my friend told me she didn't want me to be positive, I thought I was all alone, but the truth was there were plenty of people in my life who wanted to help and encourage me (like my grandpa!); I just hadn't been spending much time with them. I was keeping them on the periphery.

You might have to look beyond your inner circle to find the people who can fill some of these roles.

Think about the people you know peripherally at work or church or in your community. Is there someone you might want to get to know better? Or maybe you need to meet some new people. Is there a mastermind group in your community you can join? What about a book club? Is there a hobby you've been wanting to try? Is there a Facebook group or online forum of people doing that hobby? Always wanted to try your hand a cake decorating? Take a class at the local community college and meet some people that way.

If you'd like to get support directly from me, enroll in my DIY coaching program, Unlock Your 5-Star Future. If you're done messing around, tired of feeling stuck, and ready to supercharge your progress, this is the path for you. If you think I've included a lot of strategies in this book, wait until you see what I've done in my course. Go to becomingfutureyou.com/unlock to enroll and start making progress today.

You can find people to support you. You just need to look. (You find what you look for, remember?)

2. KNOW WHEN TO LET IT BE EASY

I know what you're thinking...

Mel, you've been going on and on about how this is going to be work, and now you're telling me to let it be easy?

Letting something be easy isn't about being lazy or careless; it's about prioritizing.

In addition to being a Master Procrastinator, I was also an expert on putting my best energy where it didn't belong. Let's say I planned to work on my business on Saturday, which was the only time I felt like I could ignore my clients and do something that mattered to me, but then we got invited to a (somewhat mandatory) family potluck. I'd accept the invite and then have a conversation with myself that went something like this:

It's fine; I'll just make a box of mac and cheese. That'll only take 15 minutes.

But if I'm going to make boxed mac and cheese, I might as well throw a little shredded cheese in there.

And if I'm going to do that, I should probably cook a few extra noodles to go with the extra cheese.

And you know what… it's not too much trouble to throw it in the oven and make baked mac and cheese. Everyone knows that's so much better.

Well shoot, if I'm going to do that, I should probably throw in a can of cheese soup and put some breadcrumbs on top. That'll be delicious!

Only I didn't have any breadcrumbs or cheese soup, and I'd end up running to the store and spending two hours making baked mac and cheese from scratch when I had started the day intending to work on my business. And the only person who would have even noticed the difference in the results… was me! Everyone at the potluck would've been fine with boxed mac and cheese and had no idea I'd contemplated making baked mac and cheese instead.

> Letting it be easy means deciding which responsibilities in your life need to get the boxed-mac-and-cheese level of effort and which deserve the gourmet baked dish.

Do you really need to fold that fitted sheet perfectly? Or do you need to take time for a workout?

Do you need to spend thirty minutes every night picking up the toys in your kid's room? Or do you need to kiss them good night and go work on your book?

Do you need to drive halfway across town to go to three different grocery stores to get the best deals? Or do you need to spend some quality time with your partner?

Not everything can get your best effort and energy; you only have so much of that to go around. So if we're talking about something that doesn't matter in the grand scheme of becoming Future You, ask yourself the question:

What would this look like if I let it be easy?

3. FIND REASONS TO BE GRATEFUL

When I moved from the Midwest to the South Carolina coast, I was absolutely fascinated by how there was water everywhere. I couldn't go anywhere without crossing at least six bridges. And don't even get me started on the delight I found in watching the drawbridges go up and down. I'm sure I was the only person sitting in that long line of traffic, clapping her hands instead of cursing the delay.

Gratitude has a host of scientifically proven benefits from helping you achieve your goals faster to strengthening your relationships to deepening your spiritual practice to improving your sleep, but they all boil down to something so simple:

Gratitude makes you feel good.

Think about the last time you were on vacation and you were so glad you weren't at work. Or the last time your partner made you laugh so hard you almost peed your pants and you thought, "I'm so happy I have this person." Or the last time you took a bite of your favorite food and thought, "This is a piece of heaven."

How did that make you feel when you noticed something you were enjoying?

It felt good, right?

But Mel! I can't go on vacation and eat chocolate cake and spend time with my honey all day every day.

Sure, but you can find reasons to be grateful in all areas of your life if you look for them. You find what you look for, remember?

Gratitude comes from noticing how something is better than it used to be or better than it could be. It comes from appreciating something for what it is right now.

Maybe you don't like your job, but you can still be grateful for your really funny coworker who always makes you smile and your comfortable chair that allows you to take a post-lunch nap every day and the way the office manager always lets you leave early to attend your kid's soccer games.

Oh, and you can be grateful for the way the job pays you and supports your lifestyle. And while you're at it, you could learn to stop sighing when you say, "I guess I'm lucky I have a job at all."

You don't have to keep that job, you know. You can be grateful for parts of it and still look for something else.

Gratitude is not the same as complacency.

I used to think being grateful would turn me into a lazy person. I thought the only way I could motivate myself to do anything was by focusing on how terrible things were. I couldn't have been more wrong.

Let me ask you… are you more likely to work on your dreams when you feel good or when you're crying about how awful your life is? Are you more likely to work on setting up your Etsy store when you feel terrible or when you feel hopeful? Are you more likely to make a salad for dinner when you're feeling optimistic or when you hate everything?

Right.

You're more likely to work on your goals when you treat yourself kindly. You're more likely to become Future You when you feel good about yourself and your life. You can't browbeat yourself into improvement. Several of my coaching clients have insisted that this isn't the case. As we've worked together on improving their self-talk, looking for reasons to be grateful, noticing their progress, and not cracking the whip all day every day though, they've discovered they are not, in fact, lazy. They realize that they will continue working without having to bully themselves into it.

Gratitude helps you become Future You.

Gratitude doesn't mean never getting angry. It doesn't mean walking around with rose-colored glasses. You can be grateful for the way Mr. Snugglebottom, your cat, purrs when he's sitting in your lap and a few minutes later get frustrated that he just ripped a giant hole in your favorite blanket. *Dangit, Mr. Snugglebottom! Not again.*

Gratitude comes in all shapes and sizes. You can be grateful for big things and small things. You can be grateful for your spouse and grateful for your comfy pajama pants. You can be grateful for your coffee and grateful that your adult child has finally stopped making such terrible choices.

Gratitude comes from noticing what's good in your life and *feeling* truly delighted by it. Gratitude is nothing without the feeling. So if you sigh and say, "I mean, I'm grateful for this car because someone in a third world country would be lucky to have it" but inside, you're thinking about what a rust bucket it is and how embarrassed you are to still be driving it… that's not gratitude.

Notice what's good in your life and let yourself feel enchanted by it.

Imagine Mel driving over a drawbridge, looking at the water all around, and saying in giddy delight, "I can't believe I get to live here!" Imagine your kid getting that princess dress on her birthday and immediately stripping down and putting it on. Imagine your dog meeting you at the door when you get home and peeing herself in delight that you came back! She thought you might be gone forever! That's gratitude.

The more you look for reasons to be grateful, the more you'll find, so practice. Start your morning with a little journaling every day and write down at least five reasons you're grateful. Or insist that each member of your family say a reason they're grateful before eating dinner. Or get a gratitude buddy—someone you talk to regularly who will ask you what you're grateful for and vice versa.

You find what you look for, and you can either keep a running list of all the reasons your life is awesome or all the reasons it's terrible. Which list is going to make you feel better?

4. RECOGNIZE HOW FAR YOU'VE COME

You might be getting excited about your unlimited potential and becoming Future You. You might have realized how awesome she could be and all the cool things she might experience, and that can be incredibly motivating. That's good! Hang on to that feeling, but just remember that becoming Future You takes time. It's easy to get worked up over your vision, start doing a few things, and then think…

Why is this taking so long?

As far as I know, overnight success isn't real. Even those people who seem to come into the spotlight from out of nowhere still spent some amount of time working up to that moment. They wrote the book or designed the product or learned the skill and all that took time, but we didn't see that part. We only see how they went from being no one to being "someone."

Wherever your dreams are leading you, the whole process is going to take time. And that can be So. Darn. Frustrating.

So instead of spinning out over why things aren't happening faster, you can get more enjoyment out of the journey by noticing how far you've already come. Trying to get your pottery business off the ground? Instead of being frustrated that it's taking longer than you thought, celebrate the fact that you managed to get three sales this month. Good job!

Instead of being so irritated that it's taking you approximately one thousand years to work up to walking three miles without dying, pat yourself on the back for the one mile you walked today. Well done, you!

How fast you're moving is a matter of perspective. When you're driving towards the mountains and you can see them in front of you, they seem the same distance away for hours. You start to think you'll never get there... *Are we even moving at all?* But if you look out the window at the grasses flashing by, you can see you're moving incredibly quickly in the right direction. So you know you will get there if you just keep driving.

Just like when we were talking about habits, recognizing how far you've come and getting that perspective may take tracking. Every time you make a post on social media in an effort to build your coaching business, maybe you add a paperclip to a jar or mark an X on a calendar. Or maybe you start a "pride journal" and every day you write down something you can feel good about. Maybe you tried something new or difficult or learned a lesson or achieved a small victory. Write it down.

We can't control the results we achieve, but we always control our efforts. Focus on the work you're doing instead of the results.

5. CELEBRATE YOUR WINS

While you're noticing your progress, set some finish lines you can cross in a reasonable amount of time and then celebrate crossing them. Let's say the goal is to declutter your entire house. That could take months and months and months. It's easy to lose motivation to work on goals that take so long to accomplish. So instead of waiting forever to celebrate your victory, celebrate mini victories along the way. Once you make it through four drawers in the kitchen, treat yourself to an extra cup of coffee and say, "This is my victory coffee!" If the goal is to create an online course, challenge yourself to finish the outline in two weeks. When it's done, treat yourself to movie night with your spouse and make sure your partner knows "This is a victory date!"

It's important that you note "I'm doing this thing to celebrate!" A lot of times celebrations won't be big or fancy. The only things that matter are that you enjoy them and you connect them to the finish line you crossed.

Not only is celebrating fun, it will give you a motivation boost as well.

6. DO WHAT BRINGS YOU JOY

This is a simple one. If we're talking about enjoying the journey, make sure you're doing things you truly enjoy.

Love snuggling with your pets? Do it on purpose every single day.

Love the feel of the sunshine on your skin? Get outside more often.

Love chatting with your sister? Call her.

Love playing silly games on your tablet? Get down with your game-playing self.

And while you're at it, stop calling the things you enjoy silly or stupid. Who cares if it seems silly to someone else? The only thing that matters is whether or not you enjoy it.

Think about those hobbies Future You has and start doing one of them even if you can't go all out. Maybe Future You walks on the beach every evening, but you don't live at the beach yet. No worries. Go for a walk anyway.

Make a literal, written list of things that bring light, joy, peace, fun, and delight into your life. Then start doing those things more regularly. If you struggle to come up with ways to celebrate your wins, use the joy list to come up with ideas. If you enjoy something, it will probably make a good reward for crossing a finish line.

THIS IS A JOURNEY, AND THE JOURNEY IS THE POINT

The goals and dreams and vision of Future You all add up to one thing: your version of a meaningful life. This is a journey, not a destination, so if you want to enjoy your life, *you can't wait to start enjoying your life*. Find the joy in the journey starting today.

DID YOU GET THAT? CHAPTER RECAP:

- It's not the achievements that will make your life meaningful; it's the experiences. And not just having the experiences but *enjoying* them.
- Here are some strategies to help you enjoy the process of becoming Future You:

  ☆ **Get Support:** Find mentors, allies, and sidekicks to participate in this journey with you. You may need to look outside your inner circle or on the internet to find these people.

  ☆ **Know When to Let it Be Easy:** Put your best energy into your top priorities and let the other things get the "boxed mac and cheese" level of effort. Ask yourself, "What would this look like if I let it be easy?"

☆ **Find Reasons to be Grateful:** Being grateful won't make you lazy, but it will make you feel good. And when you feel good, you're more likely to put effort into becoming Future You.

☆ **Recognize How Far You've Come:** You can't control the results, but you do control your effort. Make sure you're patting yourself on the back for the hard work you're doing.

☆ **Celebrate Your Wins:** Some goals take forever to achieve, but you can set smaller finish lines along the way and celebrate crossing them.

☆ **Do What Brings You Joy:** Snuggle with your pets, go for a walk, watch your favorite movie, wear your fuzzy pants—do something that brings joy to your heart!

LET ME ASK YOU THIS:

1. Who in your life is already supporting you in the way you'd like? Brainstorm a list.
2. How can you add more mentors, allies, sidekicks, and peers to your life? Or spend more time with the ones you have?
3. Which areas of your life have been getting the "gourmet mac and cheese" level of effort when they shouldn't be?
4. Off the top of your head, what are twenty things, experiences, or people you feel grateful for?

5. How can you do a better job recognizing your efforts instead of focusing solely on the results?

TAKE ACTION:

1. Get a gratitude buddy. Ask one friend or several if they'd be willing to start a gratitude text chain with you. You can text each other every time you're feeling grateful!
2. Set a finish line you can cross in the next two weeks and plan how you're going to celebrate once you cross it. (This might be doing your new habit a certain number of times!)
3. Make a list of things that bring you joy and commit to doing at least one of those things every single day.

CHAPTER 15: YOU ARE READY

Imagine waking up some time from now and walking around Future You's life. It's no longer just a vision but your truth. You have the relationships you desire and the health and fitness you currently seek; you enjoy your hobbies and spend time caring for your mind and spirit. You feel immense gratitude for the life you get to live.

Is your life perfect?

Of course not. You know there's no such thing. But it is a wonderful, meaningful, joyful life. It's full of people and experiences you love.

You still have room to grow and untapped potential. You're still on your journey to becoming Future You and, rather than overwhelming you, that excites you.

You are a completely different person than you were when you first picked up this book, and you're so grateful that Past You put forth the effort to change your reality.

THIS IS YOUR MOMENT.

You're ready to become Future You on purpose and with purpose. You don't need to wait. You don't need to procrastinate. You don't need to learn more. You've got the vision; all you need to do now is act on it.

YOU'RE RIGHT—YOU DON'T HAVE IT ALL FIGURED OUT

Of course you don't have clarity around every aspect of Future You's life, but even if you did none of the exercises, I promise a few bits of clarity popped into your head while you were reading. Maybe it was a habit you know Future You has, or some enemies Future You would never allow in her life, or the realization that Future You has hobbies. If you did the exercises and filled out the companion journal, you've got loads of details and a compelling picture of who Future You is. If you skipped the questions, it's not too late to download the free journal at becomingfutureyou.com/book and start filling in your answers.

Whether it's one detail or many, you've gained some clarity on who Future You is, and you're ready to start closing the gap between Present You and Future You by taking action.

All it takes is taking one single, purposeful step to start seeing a difference.

- Maybe you start walking through life asking yourself, "What would Future Me do?"
- Maybe you set a single goal based on a truth from your vision of Future You.
- Maybe you rewrite one of those limiting stories into something positive and work on changing the way you talk to yourself.
- Maybe you work on adopting a positive habit that you know Future You has.
- Maybe you start doing favors for Future You on

purpose so you can combat some of your usual sabotage.
- Maybe you take up journaling and start looking for reasons to be grateful.
- Maybe you start limiting time with your enemies and actively look for more allies.

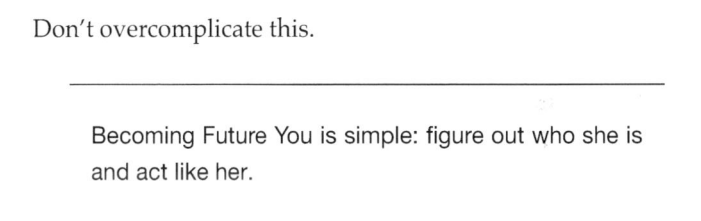

Don't overcomplicate this.

> Becoming Future You is simple: figure out who she is and act like her.

And while you're at it, learn to enjoy the journey along the way.

You might be tempted to wait for more clarity to come. It will come, but it doesn't come when you try to sit still or maintain the status quo. It comes from forward momentum. It's like driving down a highway at night. You can only see as far as the headlights shine, and it's only in driving forward that you can see farther down the path.

Even though we've been casting a vision for the nebulous future, everything you've imagined for yourself is still coming from the perspective of where you're sitting now. If you want to clarify your mission statement and uncover and rewrite more of those limiting stories and figure out what the heck Future You wants for a career, you do that by moving forward with the information you have now.

YOU'RE RIGHT—IT'S NOT THE BEST TIME

You'll never feel ready; you'll never have enough time.

Let me ask you this… how well has waiting worked so far?

Especially when we're caring for others, we're tempted to put our needs and desires on the back burner, waiting for a later that never comes. Becoming Future You is not something that takes your full focus; it's something that becomes part of how you think, and as a result, how you act. It's not something that takes away from all those people around you. When you spend time caring for yourself, you're better able to care for others.

There is no wrong time to unlock your potential. There's only your life, and it's happening every second of every day.

YOU'RE RIGHT—IT IS SCARY

Vision is great! It's like asking, "If a genie offered to grant you three million wishes, what would you wish for?" But now that you've written those things down and realized that you want them, the work ahead can seem a trifle… terrifying. Maybe you don't know how to achieve that thing, or maybe you do, but you also know the process is going to challenge you to do things you've never done before.

Here's the good news… You're normal!

Yay! Change is uncomfortable. Challenges are scary. Growth means changing and challenging yourself.

I've got a theory that comfort isn't always a positive feeling. When I was stuck, I was comfortable with my life, which is why I hadn't made any changes. I was also miserable.

Don't let the lie of comfort hold you captive.

You'll never feel ready for the challenge ahead, and change will always be scary, but you can get used to both those feelings just like you've gotten used to your life as it is.

YOU'RE RIGHT—YOU MIGHT FAIL

Failure is an important part of any hero's journey, and the biggest failures usually come before the greatest victories. It's when the sanctuary is destroyed, a beloved character is killed, the hero has been captured, the nuclear missile is headed towards the city, the team has been ripped apart… It's when all seems lost, when the heroes could just lay down and give up, that the greatest opportunities for victory appear.

It's in those moments of failure that you are able find strength you didn't know you had, stand up to your enemies and say, **"You're wrong. THIS is who I am."** And then prove it.

Failures can be your greatest opportunities for growth.

> Failures are rocket fuel in the journey of becoming Future You.

Trying to avoid failure is a losing game that will lead you away from your version of a meaningful life. Instead of letting your dreams guide you down the path, avoiding failure means using fear as your compass.

You can't become a person who has written a book unless you go through the process of writing the book, which is going to offer a myriad of possible failures and opportunities to quit. But it's only in going through the process of starting one manuscript and realizing it won't work and scrapping it and starting over and then realizing you're missing the whole point and then trying to fix it and then rewriting it again and then giving it to other people to read and realizing you're still missing something and rewriting it again that you become the kind of person who has written a book.

Or you could stop after the first or second mistake, and then you don't become the kind of person who has written a book. You become the kind of person who has started writing a book.

Learning to overcome the fears and overwhelm is what turns you into Future You, a person who knows how to move past her fears and take action anyway. You can't just snap your fingers and suddenly not be afraid anymore; you've got to practice being courageous in the face of fear. Present You has got to practice being calm and focused when confronted with overwhelm. You've got to take actions in spite of the fears and the possibility of failure.

If Future You is not a fearful procrastinator, Present You has to learn to deal with those things.

> There are no shortcuts; the only path to 5-Star Future You is through.

You'll make mistakes, but then you'll get back up. Life and other people will knock you down, and you'll get back up. You'll let fear get the best of you momentarily, but then you'll get back up. Everything that happens can be *for* you, an experience that helps you grow into Future You, as long as you get back up.

How do you get back up?

Get motivated with your WHY.

Remember why you're working on the goal or chasing the dream or trying to create a meaningful life. Who are you helping? Who needs you to become Future You?

Clarify your vision.

Visualize what success is going to look and feel and be like. Make that picture in your mind so clear you can smell the popcorn on the opening night of your movie debut.

Remember the stakes.

This is your life we're talking about here. Your one and only shot. Are you going to make it count?

Get help.

Find a mentor, enlist your allies, join my DIY coaching program... ask for help. It's not a sign of weakness; it's an indicator that you're smart enough to know the journey is better with friends.

Whatever it takes... get up.

YOU CAN DO THIS

You can live a meaningful, heroic life, but you have to combine vision and action.

You can be the hero of your own story, but heroes don't wait on the couch for good things to happen. They make a decision even if they're not sure it's the right one; they go through the doorway and they come back forever changed. Your doorway is already open. Future You is waiting for you to walk through.

Becoming Future You is simple: figure out who she is and then act like her. And while you're at it, enjoy the journey.

You've got this!

Love,

Mel

Your 5-Star Life Coach ☆

ACKNOWLEDGMENTS

I couldn't have written this book without you. Without knowing you were going to be reading it and learning from it and using the tools to change your life. Thank you for seeing it through to the end. I know Future You will be glad you did, and I can't wait to hear about your progress.

If this book helped you, it can help other people you know. Please help me get the word out by reviewing it wherever you purchased it, recommending it to your friends, talking about it on social media, asking your library to purchase a copy, buying a second copy and leaving it on your neighbor's doorstep, or getting creative with your own options! Reviews and recommendations are vital in helping a book reach readers. It's important to get this message into the hands of everyone who needs it, and that will only happen with your help.

If you'd like to be on my launch team and get early access to the next book, *Stop Sabotaging Future You* (coming in 2022) you can sign up at becomingfutureyou.com/book2.

If you want to receive regular encouragement from me in your inbox, sign up at becomingfutureyou.com/newsletter

I had a lot of help in my journey of becoming Future Mel, the Published Author, and there's no way I can quantify it in a few short paragraphs. Let me just say this: If you ever gave me a word of encouragement or a bit of advice or told me you loved me or smiled at me at a writers' conference or replied to one of my newsletters or liked one of my many pictures of my pets on Instagram—you helped. Thanks, buddy!

I owe a huge thanks to each of my Unlock Your 5-Star Future students and coaching clients, who gave me insight and feedback and said, "Yes, Mel, this works," as I tested my theories on them over the past several years. Special thanks to Jolene for allowing me to include her story in this book.

This book would not exist if Sarah Wendell had not introduced me to the concept of the three versions of You and asked me, "What would this look like if you let it be easy?" You changed my life, Sarah!

Jackie Siemann, what can I say? I'm forever grateful our weird brains found each other.

Tawdra Kandle and Lisa Hughey were instrumental in not only the creation of this book, but so many of my efforts. I'm grateful you two are my cheerleaders and brainstorming buddies! Thanks to Colleen Chrien for telling me if I finished writing this book, she would buy me a steak dinner. I hope you meant it because I'm coming to collect! Thanks to my sister, Becky Hermann, for being my gratitude buddy and for telling me, "You're fine" anytime I got stressed out.

I'm enormously grateful every day for my sweet husband who told me over and over not only did he think I could write a book but that he was sure it would be a big success. Thanks for being my greatest cheerleader, honey.

Thanks, Universe, for helping me write this book. I believe we got it right.

Manufactured by Amazon.ca
Bolton, ON